THE
VERY BEST
OF

Dear Marje

MARJORIE
PROOPS

Mirror Books is an imprint of Bookman Projects Limited.
Published by Bookman Projects Limited
The Mirror Building, 33 Holborn, London EC1P 1DQ
First published 1993
© Bookman Projects Limited
Designed and produced by Nick Kent Associates
Spirella House, Letchworth, Herts SG6 4ET

ISBN 1-898718-00-8

Printed and bound in Great Britain by
BPCC Paperbacks Ltd
Member of BPCC Ltd

CONTENTS

INTRODUCTION

IT'S the question that's familiar to every Agony Aunt: "Are all those letters you publish made up?"

In the twenty-two years since I have been the Daily Mirror's Agony Aunt, we have published several thousand. Not one of them has been invented. Every single letter has been a genuine plea for help and advice or a genuine cry of anguish or a genuine need to seek sympathy, attention or consolation.

The letters which appear in the columns of the Daily and Sunday Mirror are the tiny tip of a huge iceberg. Out of the twenty-five thousand or so letters a year which land on my desk, there's space in the newspapers only for a very small proportion of the letters readers send me.

Every reader who sends me a name and address receives a personal, often long and detailed, reply and, where appropriate, special information about, say, organisations that can give them additional help.

I contact social services departments, welfare organisations, specialist counselling services on readers' behalf. I arrange penfriends, advise about divorce, about housing, about debts. The list is as varied and as endless as the requests.

"How do you select those you print?" is a frequent question. Choosing which letters to put in the paper is, I think one of the toughest parts of my job.

I select them from among the anonymous correspondence people send. A smallish proportion of worried or embarrassed citizens are afraid to reveal their identity. Many say "I dare not give you my name and address, my husband – or wife – opens my mail..."

Some hope that if they write, say, about a rat of a boyfriend or a husband's betrayal, a letter printed in the paper will bring that rat or that defecting spouse to heel. And sometimes it actually works and a thrilled wife writes again to say "thanks, Marje, he's come back."

One of my regrets is that I don't often hear whether the advice I've dished out has, in fact, helped. Or failed to help. But when, as happens over and over again, someone says at the end of a letter "I feel a lot better for writing to you", I get an enormous sense of satisfaction and fulfilment out of doing what is a much more difficult and complex job than most people imagine.

Sometimes I'll meet a joker at a party and he'll chortle (it's almost always a he) "I bet you get a lot of saucy, sexy letters, eh?"

I have to control a strong urge to throw a hard punch at characters like this, who assume that the people writing to Agony Aunts are either harmless nutters or have nothing better to do with their time than scribble a couple of pages of trivial rubbish.

In fact the vast majority of people who write to me have serious and difficult problems and no one to whom they can turn in times of stress and anxiety except a stranger they'll never meet. That, perhaps, is one of the bonuses of writing to an Agony Aunt.

You are not compelled to confront someone you know, like a doctor, perhaps, or a social worker. You may be afraid to trust friends with intimate secrets. You can't talk to parents who might not understand or to other relatives who might be judgmental or condemnatory. You need a stranger who won't be likely to pass judgement but whose training and experience in counselling seems safe.

These are the reasons, I believe, why thousands of troubled people seek help from objective Agony Aunts Strangers indeed – yet dedicated to helping as best they can those who write to them. When selecting the letters which appear in this book, I went through files going back years. Basically, problems haven't changed very much because people haven't changed much in the past twenty years or so.

But there is clear evidence of a few fascinating changes in society and in attitudes. Particularly so far as women are concerned.

When I first began the Dear Marje column, it was customary for me to receive letters from wives telling me how they submitted sexually to their husbands.

They'd say, "I submit to him about twice a month" or "he expects me to submit to him three times a week"... or twice a night or once a month...

Now I'd be amazed if a woman wrote and told me she has to submit to a man. Happily women have ceased to be submissive, unless of course they are into playing sado-masochistic games with their man, when they do it for fun and sexual kicks.

But they're a different breed from the "yes dear, certainly dear" wives who used to send me pathetic letters about their bullying partners.

Today's women are fighting back. Their self-image is stronger. They are much more positive and demanding and aggressive. Too aggressive for their own good, I sometimes think, though they'd argue with me about that.

Other changes I've seen include the big increase in the number of broken marriages, the alarming rise in the divorce rate and in the number of one-parent families struggling to rear children on their meagre state benefits.

I've seen crime rising unstoppably, kids and teenagers totally out of control and child abuse almost a national pastime. And I get letters from frightened victims or distraught parents and because Agony Aunts don't come equipped with Magic Wands, there's little I can do other than offer comfort and support. I have also seen a dramatic increase in domestic violence, mostly by men against women, though now women are beginning to get in on the act. It's that aggression again.

One other significant change has been in attitudes towards homosexuals. After the law relating to male homosexuality was reformed, more and more gay men felt brave enough to "come out" and admit to their sexual preferences and to be seen publicly with their partners.

But while society is perhaps a bit more tolerant than it was, there's still plenty of prejudice, which causes great pain and problems. A lot of them come my way and happily, I've been able to sort many of these problems out.

I shuddered though, when I opened the letter one young man in his early twenties sent me. He described how he'd gone to his room and was watching a gay video when his mother walked in, gave him a hiding and called the police. That boy wasn't easy to counsel. But the one who really needed serious counselling was the gay man's mother.

There are a few lighter moments in my day, when people describe incidents that give me a good laugh. Like the wife who told me how she spotted a hunky odd job man up a ladder and how she left her bedroom window open after the old man had gone to work and how the odd job man popped in and performed a very skilled odd job during his lunch break.

And I sniggered, though perhaps I shouldn't have, at the letter from a confused husband who described how he'd got home early from work one day and he went upstairs to discover his wife and the next-door neighbour on the bed, not exactly fully clothed, and they told him they'd only been testing the springs on the new bed.

Most of my letters, though, are no joke. I am more likely at the end of a working day to go home saddened and depressed by the awful pain people inflict on each other, than I am laughing about breaking in bed springs. And if, when you've read this book's selection of the letters I've received over the years, you think "maybe Marje could help me too" – a letter to the Daily Mirror or Sunday Mirror will reach me and you can be sure I'll do my best to help.

Conned by a cruel rat

Dear Marje

Three months ago, I met the man of my dreams. He's really good-looking and when he told me he loved me I was over the moon.

One night he was driving us home from a club and he stopped the car and we had sex.

I didn't want to. I was scared because I'm not yet 16 and I know it's not legal, but he said if I really loved him, I would and I gave in and we made love in the back of the car. The next day he rang me and said that he was sorry about what had happened, he'd lost his head, but he was engaged and he couldn't see me again.

He said I should forget it and forget him and not talk to anyone about it. I haven't heard from him since.

Now I've missed a period and I think I must be pregnant because I feel very weird. I don't know what to do. I feel used and ashamed and frightened. I haven't told anyone. Please can you give me some advice? Should I ring him up and tell him?

Says Marje

I know exactly what I'd do to this charmer if I could get close enough to him – my treatment would somewhat curtail his sexual activities.

But let's not waste too much time on him.

You must try to shed your feeling of shame, for although you realised that his love-making was illegal, you were hardly a match for an experienced man putting the ultimate pressure on a girl too young to exercise any judgment.

Used you were. It's the old, old blackmailing story, one that always pays off for the man.

How many girls, I wonder, have melted when a man says

11

"prove you really love me"? It's the cheapest way of getting sex. I emphasise the word cheap. I'm finding it hard to cool my anger to try to give you some practical advice.

First, don't spend the price of a phone call to tell this rat he got you pregnant.

He'll deny it and it'll be your word against his. He has no conscience and he's not going to risk his girlfriend finding out what kind of a man she's planning to marry.

I assume you don't want to have this baby. If you did, you'd need to tell your mother and get her help and support. You'd have to face the problems of being a very young single mum. You might think I seem to be promoting the idea of abortion. Actually, I'm not. Abortion can result in a long and painful trauma of guilt.

I am simply spelling out the options, for there's no easy or happy solution for you – victim as you were of an unprincipled, unscrupulous man.

If you decide to have the termination, ring Brook Helpline on 071-617 8000 for advice. It's a 24-hour recorded information service.

I wish you had someone with whom you could share your terror and your panic, but Brook will help you to deal with the consequences of the car ride which ended in such misery for a frightened, lonely girl.

Saucy sir hasn't learnt his lesson

Dear Marje

About four years ago a supply teacher came to our school. I was 14 and he was 22 and it wasn't long before we had sex.

I was a virgin but he told me that he'd take care of everything. We made love often and one weekend he took me to a hotel where we had almost non-stop sex.

Then I found I was pregnant. He paid for an abortion and made me promise not to tell anyone.

Soon after, he left the school and although I was heartbroken, I was kind of relieved. I knew what we did was dangerous.

12

Now, believe it or not, he is back at the school, which I left last year, as a permanent teacher and my young sister has seen him kissing and touching up one of the other young kids.

I am in a terrible state, not knowing whether I should write to the head about what he did to me.

Would it get me and him into serious trouble? Please, please advise me.

Says Marje

Let me put your mind at rest about any trouble you might get into as a result of this teacher's appaling behaviour.

You will not be held responsible for what happened to you.

You were a child of 14, a victim of a man old enough to know he was committing an offence against a minor under the legal age of consent.

If it had been discovered at the time it could certainly have got him into trouble with the law.

Why, I wonder, has your young sister now confided in you about her fears for this other child? Did your family learn what happened to you?

Or is it that your sister simply feels that you, older and wiser, would know what to do.

I hope that you have been able to take someone close whom you trust into your confidence – for the abortion, huge relief as it must have been at the time, remains in your mind.

Abortion almost always leaves a trauma from which some women never recover.

Ideally, a girl in your situation should have received counselling.

But failing that, your mother could have consoled you, or a sympathetic doctor could have helped you to come to terms with what happened.

But never for a moment forget that you were a child victim of an adult man who seduced you and used you, lied to you and abandoned you.

There's no reason for you to feel a trace of guilt and I hope these words of mine will help to dispel any you may still feel. You MUST ring the head of your old school and tell him or her about your sister's suspicions. Say you've very good personal reasons to believe they could be justified. I don't think you need mention the abortion. But I think you could reveal that this teacher had sex with you and you'd be prepared to talk about it confidentially.

As you should, to protect other kids whose lives could be as damaged by him as yours was.

Outraged by a nude photo of dad

Dear Marje

My parents are in their mid-40s and I know they still have sex, which is quite horrible enough.

But I found something really yukky in my mother's bedroom drawer the other day.

It was a picture of my dad posing in the nude. It was so disgusting, it made me want to puke. I think they must be perverted or something. Having sex at their age is OK, I suppose, but all the other stuff is repulsive.

They're always giggling and touching each other up and making really suggestive remarks.

I hate to bring my friends home to see the way they carry on. The nude picture is absolutely the last straw.

I think it's time they started acting their age and being more dignified.

Should I drop hints – or come right out and tell them what I think? I am 14, by the way.

Says Marje

What were you doing, rummaging around in your mother's bedroom drawer? How would you feel if you discovered she'd been prowling round in your room, invading your privacy? Outraged, I guess, and rightly so. Just as she and your father would be outraged at your darned cheek.

Your parents' sex life is none of your business and if your mother keeps a photo of your dad in a drawer beside her bed it's because she likes the way he looks, with or without his clothes on.

Look up the word "perverted" in your dictionary. You'll find it doesn't apply to your parents. They share a wholehearted and wholesome enjoyment of sex which is an expression of the way they love each other, and it's great.

I hope you'll have similar fun and games one day with someone you love and who loves you.

What is especially good about your mum and dad's marriage is that they're so frank and open.

Don't you realise how lucky you are to have them, rather than parents who fight and quarrel and hit each other? Now that's what I call repulsive.

I think some of those friends you're so reluctant to bring home might well envy you. But I understand why you are embarrassed about all that passion.

Only rarely can children face up to their parents' sexuality. Yet without their sex, you wouldn't have been born. And without their love for each other and their touching demonstrations of it, you'd be a much sadder girl.

I hope you won't be impertinent enough to tell them what you think. They might just tell you what they think about your snooping.

Don't ever do it again. You might find more than you bargain for, such as love letters they've exchanged – which are strictly for their eyes only.

She longs for private 'lessons' after school

Dear Marje

I am 17, still at school working for my A-levels. Recently I started extra coaching from one of the teachers and I am finding it hard to cope with my feelings about him.

He's about 40, married with a daughter around my age and I am in love with him. He is a wonderfully warm person and I can talk to him as if I was his equal. He doesn't treat me like I'm a child, the way most teachers do.

He has a great sense of humour and we laugh as well as work together and I hope you won't put me down as foolish when I tell you I truly love him. I no longer have

15

16 THU

any interest in the boys of my own age I used to go with, I can't even talk to them now. There's no one I can discuss this with, though I'm terribly tempted to tell him how I feel.

Although I want to please him, my work is suffering and so am I. I can't sleep for thinking of him and wanting him. Please can you help me?

Says Marje

The reason why your teacher doesn't treat you like a child is because he's well aware that you are not one. Only too well aware, I suspect.

I also suspect he is beginning to be a bit wary of you. Or he would be if he's got an ounce of commonsense along with his academic qualifications.

They don't always go hand in hand, more's the pity. There's many an older married man whose commonsense goes walkies when a nubile love-struck girl comes within easy grasp. You are certainly within your teacher's grasp, willing and eager as you would be to fall into his arms if he were daft enough to open them out to you.

I am not going to scoff at the notion that you love this man. I can well believe that you do. You are a mature, sensible analytical girl and I can see why boys of your own age seem boring and foolish compared to your smooth-talking teacher.

I also get the feeling you've already had some sexual experience with a spotty adolescent or two. And that by comparison, the older man seems immensely sexy and desirable.

But I fear you are about to learn one of the hardest lessons so many women must learn, even at the early age of 17.

Which is that while you may yearn and ache for forbidden love, you must keep your hands to yourself and your feelings secret. Give in to the temptation to tell him you're wild about him and he'll be off. Or I earnestly hope for his sake and yours, that he would be.

If he was foolish enough to fulfil your dreams for a few secret stolen hours, he'd rapidly junk you at the first sign of danger and you'd soon have another teacher coaching you through your A-levels. But you know all this, don't you?

As you say, you're not a child. But it's a pity you have had to learn grown-up lessons so young.

This mum wants to divorce her daughter

Dear Marje

When I read all these stories about 14-year-old children seeking "divorces" from their parents, I laugh bitterly. How about a law to give parents of rude, lazy, selfish children the right to get a "divorce" from them?

My 14-year-old daughter is frankly, a pain. She comes and goes as she pleases.

When I ask her where she's off to, she says "OUT" and bangs the door. Her room is a pit. She openly sleeps with her boyfriend. The other morning I came downstairs to find them both near naked asleep on the settee. When her father threatens to cut down her pocket money, she tells him to f***g stuff it.

She works weekends in a shop so she can be independent. It might sound harsh but I often ask myself if I really do love this creature I gave birth to. I'm glad to have got this off my chest. It has helped me even though I realise, of course, that you can't.

Says Marje

It's a brave and honest mother who can openly express the anger and frustration countless parents feel when they try to deal with offspring like yours.

I suppose every generation of parents has to cope with bolshie, bloody-minded kids, though it does seem to me that today's lot have brought defiance to a fine art.

Some parents simply shrug and give up, knowing when they're beaten. Then they suffer endless pangs of guilt and spend sleepless nights wondering if it's all their fault.

Others simply sigh, hoping that one magical day they'll

awake to find the little monsters they spawned have turned overnight into little angels with clean necks who say please and thank you.

Dreams of reform of today's foul-mouthed, rude and self-centred children are unlikely to come true. Children are subject to influences beyond our control. Like dirty videos, questionable TV progs and sleazy films.

At 14 they can easily pass for 18 and drink in pubs. They can, and do, smoke. Thirteen and 14-year-old girls get pregnant – parents are lucky if boyfriends use condoms. It's a gloomy depressing picture isn't it?

But I don't think we should forget that for every young rebel, there are a lot of civilised teenagers who brush their teeth and do their homework, who don't go all the way with their boyfriends.

And they are nice to their mothers and fathers and still think of sex as something boring they learn in the biology class.

The generation gap has always been with us, as your wild girl will one day discover. Meanwhile, I think you can feel confident that she'll soon grow up and realise on which side her bread is buttered and where to turn if she's in trouble. Then, I guess, you'll know you do love the little monster.

For underneath all that defiance there's an insecure kid struggling to get away from her mother's lifestyle to one she thinks, right now, is the smart one.

And only because it's so different from yours.

Best friend stole her Romeo

Dear Marje

I am a girl aged 14 and I am in love with a boy at school who is 16.

I have been out with him three times and I am really serious about him and I was very upset when he didn't suggest another date.

He said he had to work for his exams. I told my best friend, who said she would have a talk to him to find out what was going on. Now he is going out with her. They are always together and I am very depressed. She has really let me down and that's after swearing we would always be friends and tell each other everything. I have an idea she lets him go all the way, which I wouldn't because I am scared of getting pregnant and of Aids.

Do you think I should have it out with her? Or with him?

I feel like telling everyone at school about the way they've let me down. I would like to have your opinion, please.

Says Marje

It's tough that you've been forced to learn some very painful lessons at such a young age, though you probably reckon you are, in fact, quite mature.

Actually you are indeed more mature than many of your contemporaries who do not have as sensible an attitude to sex as you do. Perhaps the simple reason why your ex-boyfriend moved over to your best friend was because she's less responsible than you are and lets this Romeo go as far as he likes.

I hope she insists he uses a condom. Still, that's her worry now, not yours.

The horrible lesson you've learned is that best friends can and do betray the people who trust them. And men are often faithless creatures who don't know the first thing about loyalty.

Another lesson you are in the process of learning, though you won't realise it right now, is that broken hearts do in time heal. Especially when those hearts are only 14 years old. I'll expect you to be cured in a couple of weeks or so.

Meanwhile, let's consider what you should do now. Should you have it out with her or him? Or let the whole school know what a couple of dirty rats they are? I don't think you should do any of these things. Your best plan is to behave with dignified silence. Having it out and exposing your hurt to the world could simply make you look pathetic.

Whatever you do won't change anything. Your erstwhile best friend and this boy will still be going together – at least until he gets cheesed off with her and finds someone else.

And telling everyone won't be a punishment for them, only for yourself. This unhappy affair will, I hope, teach you to be extra specially choosy about making the right choices. And I hope the friends you choose from now on will prove that there are plenty of decent ones around who'll keep their word and won't betray your friendship or your love.

Haunted by her sad daughter's home truth

Dear Marje

I recently came across my teenage daughter's diary in her room. In it she describes her terrible loneliness and depression that is driving her to thoughts of suicide.

She blames it on her unhappy childhood which, she says, lacked warmth and affection.

I can't describe my pain on reading her words.

I have always thought we were a close and stable family and though we're not materially rich, we have been generous with our time and our love.

My daughter is going to university in the autumn but unlike her elder sister, she is moody and introverted and it's hard for her to make friends. In fact, she's quite like me. I am finding it very difficult to cope with the guilt I feel about invading her privacy and my hopeless failure as a parent.

Says Marje

Will it help you to accept the fact – for fact it is – that very few good parents escape the sort of torture you are now enduring? Only good parents care as deeply as you do.

It's the indifferent ones, the casual ones, the selfish ones who'd shrug and say "she'll get over it, it's merely an adolescent phase". Actually it probably is, but because you are so distressed about your daughter's diary confession, you can't see it that way.

There are no doubt several reasons for her misery. Fear of going to university where, because she's not an outgoing girl, she may dread loneliness. Fear, perhaps, of failing her family's expectations. Maybe there's unspoken jealousy of her livelier sister. You are your daughter's scapegoat. All of us need one at some time or another. We blame our partners, the Government, the weather – anything or anyone who can be held to be responsible for our misery.

For children, the easiest targets to blame are parents.

As parents, we have to take it, the way our parents had to take it from us and the way our children themselves will one day have to take it.

Even the best and most loving parents, like you, make mistakes, wrong decisions, wrong judgments.

That doesn't mean you are a bad, unloving mother.

I am sorry you saw your girl's diary because it has made you feel so guilty.

But since you did, all you can do now is try to boost her confidence and try – subtly – to be a little more of a chummy mummy. And console yourself with the thought that most teenagers, emotional as they are, dramatise themselves.

One last thought: Maybe she's been ditched by a boyfriend.

She'd blame everyone for that – you, her father, her sister, God. But never, of course, herself.

Give thanks that you're around to be her scapegoat.

She wants to swap her mum

Dear Marje

I wish you were my mother instead of the horrible one I've got. I am the youngest of three girls. I am nearly 14. They wanted a boy and they've always taken it out on me for being a girl.

My mother has had post-natal depression ever since I was born, and she takes it out on me.

She has to have medication and I got so fed up with her, I took some of her pills and there was a right ruckus about that. I think it's because of her that I get into trouble at school. Horrible teachers are forever getting at me for being rude and looking a mess.

The other day, my mother actually hit me in public. I was really humiliated. I am fed up. I hope you don't think I am boring. All my mother cares about is what her posh

26 T1+J

friends think. I have thought about running away, but perhaps you can suggest how I can get the better of her.

Says Marje

If I was your mother, I bet you'd hate me just as much as the one you've got. Even more, probably, on account of I'd be giving you long, boring lectures telling you to think how other people feel sometimes instead of always thinking about your own feelings. Most offspring think mothers are a pain in the neck. Likewise, most teachers seem to be horrible.

It's only when you're really old, maybe in your thirties, you can look back and realise they weren't so bad and they did their best to get some sense and knowledge into you.

Certainly, if I was your mum I'd be out of my mind with worry if you took some of my medication, because I'd realise you did it to get back at me.

I'm interested in your theory about your parents being nasty to you because you're a daughter and not a son. You could be right, but I think that if they are as nasty as you say, it might be because you are so recalcitrant. Look that up in your dictionary.

Also look up "rude", "mess" and "depression". What I'm trying to say is that it's time you learned there are two sides, at least, to every situation.

Your mum gets one of her attacks of depression, you are bloody-minded. She feels too lousy to reason with you patiently, you're too into your own feelings to care about hers.

But there's a chance of making things better, if only you can see that no-one is perfect. And that definitely includes me.

Stick to the mum you've got and be sad that she's sick and glad you're a girl. It takes a woman to understand another one. Maybe you are the strong one in the family. If you're not now, I'm certain you could be if you gave it serious thought.

They must tell their teacher

Dear Marje

Please, please print this letter. My friends and I, who are all 14, are desperate. We are afraid one of our friends

might kill herself. Last week she took eight paracetamol pills, she eats a lot and makes herself sick and she looks awful. She says she hates her mum and dad, though we think they seem all right.

The other day she said she had been raped but she won't give us any details. She is always telling lies.

We feel we should do something to try to help her, but what? She'd never forgive us if she knew we'd written to you. Could she be saying all these things to get noticed?

As her friends and schoolmates, we are very anxious to do whatever we can to help her.

Some of the girls think we should talk to our teacher. The snag about that is she'd know it was us and she would never speak to us again.

Please help us, we can't stop worrying about her.

Says Marje

This unhappy girl is truly very lucky indeed to have a bunch of friends like you.

I expect you are all aware that most teenagers go through sticky patches. It's usually to do with the hormones becoming active and the personality changes that take place as a result of these changes.

Some people are lucky enough to feel no ill effects, but you are right to be worried about your friend.

I'm a bit baffled about her mum and dad. If they're as okay as you think they are, I wonder why they haven't noticed how ill she looks.

If she's bingeing food and throwing up, she has an eating disorder called bulima nervosa. It's curable, but your friend would have to be persuaded to seek help.

The other things you describe – the lies, the rape fantasy, the pills – are all symptoms of her condition.

I've said the rape is a fantasy, but I could be wrong about that. She may indeed have been sexually abused or raped.

But true or not, the lies, the suicide threats and attempts, her hatred of her parents, indicate that she is a very disturbed girl.

And yes, you should talk to your teacher who, I'm sure, will respect your confidence. She's in a position to have a discreet chat with your friend's parents. Your teacher will know what steps can be taken. As a responsible adult, she'll be anxious about her pupil and she won't dish the dirt on any of you.

She'll recognise the symptoms as a desperate cry for help and I hope that your friend's cries won't have been in vain.

They haven't, in fact, because you, her friends, have listened and taken action.

I suggest you show this page to your teacher. She might like to have the name and address of an organisation which can help people with bulima nervosa.

It is The Eating Disorders Association, Sackville Place, 44 Magdalen Street, Norwich, Norfolk NR3 1JU. The helpline number is 0603 621414.

Sick of a soppy lover

Dear Marje

I have been having regular sexual intercourse with a 27-year-old man I've known for six months. I am just 16. I know I was off the wall to get into this, but he's a bit pushy.

He's really slushy, calling me his dearest sweetheart – he sounds like my gran. He says he loves me and wants to marry me but I'm not into all that sentimental stuff.

My problem is how to get rid of him. I don't mind the sex, though he often tries to make me do oral and other things I don't like much.

He's not violent but when I tell him to pack it in he cries and sobs and I feel guilty and mean, as if I'm responsible.

It's hard for me to avoid him because we live in the same block of flats and he waits around for me.

Should I tell my mum, who has a boyfriend around his age? Or have you any idea how I can junk him without hurting his feelings, because he's a nice man and maybe I did lead him on.

Says Marje

I have strong doubts about whether this man is as nice as you say. My opinion of him is a lot less charitable. Is it nice for a 27-year-old man to have a sexual relationship with someone under the legal age of consent?

I don't think a nice man would try emotional blackmail to induce a girl to participate in oral sex and "other things" which you haven't spelled out but which I can guess.

Nor would a genuinely nice man hang around your flat, unnerving you in his very nice way.

A man of his age who turns on the tap to try to make a vulnerable girl amenable to his seedy desires is a particularly nasty specimen and you need feel neither guilt nor compunction about telling him to shove off.

You can do it nicely, of course, by explaining that though you think he's great, you're not ready for a permanent relationship and it is positively no go.

I did consider suggesting you tell him the age gap of 11 years might count against any chance of a long-lasting marriage but then I remembered your mum and her boyfriend. There's probably a similar age gap there, so that argument could collapse.

I think you should leave your mum out of this for the time being. But if the man continues to pester you then ask her for help.

I wouldn't go into too much detail about your sex life, if I were you. There's no point in elaborating on the oral and other demands. She might give him the good hiding he deserves.

But there's no harm in mentioning to this man that you don't want to have to tell your mum because you fear the resulting punch-up.

He'll probably burst into tears when you say it's got to be goodbye forever. But don't feel guilty or pity him. He's been the guilty one from the start.

Get knotted

Dear Marje

I am middle-aged and divorced and I have been living with the woman I love, also divorced, for about 12 years.

Recently I decided it was time I made an "honest woman" of her and said we should get married. She refused. I simply couldn't believe it.

She's been nagging me to get married for years and I thought it would make her happy to tie the knot at last.

She's willing to go on living with me, she says, but she wants to be free. I've argued that she's not free anyway, any more than I am. We already live as man and wife.

I have a feeling that her two teenage daughters are behind all this. They've never liked me and frankly I don't like them, either. They are lazy, arrogant and selfish. But I haven't let my feelings show.

It won't be long before they leave home to lead their own lives and for my part, it'll be good riddance. How can I persuade their mother, without slagging them off, that I, not they, am her future?

Says Marje

I fear there's a touch of arrogance about you too. You shack up with this lady and you ignore her pleas to legalise the union. Then, for reasons you've not made clear, you suddenly decide to make what you insultingly describe as an "honest woman" of her.

If you said that to her when you made your unromantic proposal, I'm surprised she didn't tell you to bog off. But I am not surprised she won't marry you. You offered her marriage like you were doing her a big favour.

I daresay you meant that "honest woman" remark as a joke, but it is not the sort of joke that someone in your partner's situation would find funny.

You blame her daughters for putting the boot in and you may

26

well be right. But however much those girls detest you, I doubt if they could have influenced her.

No, I think she's simply fed up with your attitude, bestowing, as you did, the offer of a plain gold hand like you are doing her a great honour. But don't despair. I reckon if you put yourself out and try wooing her, she could relent when she figures she's punished you enough.

Don't kid yourself that she's not aware how much you detest her daughters. And how much they detest you. I'm sure they've done their best to put the poison in, but it's obvious they've not succeeded otherwise she'd surely have left you before now.

It's just as well you've managed to avoid the temptation to tell their mother you can't stand them. For you are, in effect, their stepfather.

If you are more tactful and sensitive to your partner's feelings and tell her you want her to marry you because you love her to death, with luck you'll be a bridegroom before the year is out.

His marriage terrors

Dear Marje

I am getting married in three weeks' time – unless I chicken out before the big day.

But I am not the overwrought bride having the vapours every five minutes. I am the overwrought bridegroom.

My wife-to-be is calm and organised. She is a successful business-woman and anyone would think she is arranging a conference, rather than her wedding.

I am the one who is suffering from pre-marriage nerves and although this letter may seem a bit jokey, I am deadly serious. There have been all the usual family arguments. The two mothers are on the point of murdering each other, the two fathers go off to the pub to escape and my girlfriend goes to work as usual.

She accuses me of being a spineless wimp because I've admitted my fears.

Are there many men to your knowledge, like me or is it only women who indulge in this pre-marriage terror?

Says Marje

I don't think women have exclusive rights to the wedding-day fears and tensions you describe. It does, though, seem that more females get in a state.

It is par for the confetti-strewn course for the mothers to fight like demented cats and it isn't difficult to understand why.

Both mothers are apprehensive about their offspring's future.

Both are secretly convinced that their children could have found better partners.

And both become irritated with the male members of the cast, including the groom, who is regarded as hardly more than an accessory.

I am sure every responsible man facing marriage feels as you do. Very few can contemplate the future without misgivings and I don't think that's such a bad thing.

Indifference to responsibilities or over-confidence can only lead to problems once the honeymoon is over.

I imagine your pre-wedding nerves are due to a certain insecurity. I am not surprised.

You are marrying a very strong woman who might well be the controlling partner.

Your marriage could be a power-struggle. Even before your beloved says "I do", she has dismissed you as a wimp.

A cruel jibe, that, guaranteed to wound.

There are still three weeks to go. Not long, but long enough, I figure, for you to establish some ground rules and make sure the goalposts are properly positioned.

If you can't, you might indeed be wise to chicken out now, even though it would mean nervous breakdowns all round.

I am sure your rejected bride-to-be would soon be sending out brisk wedding cancellation cards between her business conferences. And I get the feeling that in the long run few hearts would be broken, certainly not yours.

She can't love this perfect guy

Dear Marje

I was a really wild teenager, into drugs and drink and sex. I'd had two abortions before I was 17. My parents were worried out of their minds, they couldn't understand why I acted the way I did. I think it's because I had a very repressive, strict upbringing as an only child. I went to college and got a quite decent job.

I honestly regret the pain and worry I gave my parents. I can see now how it must have nearly finished them and I vowed to myself that I'd make it up to them.

Their dearest wish is that I marry a nice steady guy and they were immensely relieved when I met one. I am now engaged to him but I don't think I'm in love with him, though I'd like to be. My parents reckon he's perfect.

He's never taken anything stronger than an aspirin and a couple of glasses of wine is his idea of living it up. He's only had a sketchy, censored account of my past but even before we marry I feel trapped. Yet if I ditch him it'll be one more terrible blow to my parents.

Says Marje

Ditch him right away. If you marry him, inevitably you'll mess up his life as well as your own.

The worst possible reason for anyone to marry is to please parents. Yours have had more than enough to contend with without having to pick up the pieces of a broken marriage.

It's a noble gesture to marry this man to make up to your parents for all the grief you gave them. But your judgment isn't much better now than it was in your wild teens.

There's a note of scorn in your description of the man who loves you. Why should you be so sarcastic because he's never done drugs and is only a very modest drinker? You're contemptuous about him even before you walk down the aisle with him.

Of course it would be wonderful for your mother and father to see you walking beside him to the strains of the Wedding March. It would be a proud day for them.

From one brief sentence in your letter you put the blame for your wild past squarely on their shoulders and I think you may have a point.

But it's easy enough, in retrospect, to blame someone else for your own shortcomings. Poor parents. They get the blame if they're too indulgent just as they do if they're too repressive. They can rarely win. Going back to the man you'd like to talk yourself into loving. I have to remind you that love isn't an intellectual exercise. You can't think or will yourself into it. It is an emotional commitment. You either feel it or you don't. And you don't.

Give him back his engagement ring and bid him a regretful farewell. And don't worry too much about your parents' disappointment. They must have got used to that.

It's better they're disappointed now than in a few years hence when you will add to the broken marriage statistics, as you undoubtedly will if you marry a man you secretly despise.

Wedding night nerves of a pensioner bride

Dear Marje

I realise that sex is something the young think belongs exclusively to them, but they are wrong.

I have just picked up my bus pass and I am as excited about my future as any teenage bride-to-be.

I am engaged to a 73-year old widower but as we get closer to our wedding I am beginning to worry.

You may find it hard to believe that a woman of my age has never had a lover, but it's a fact.

I was engaged once before, in my twenties, but we never went beyond a few kisses. I'd like the answers to a couple of questions, please. Can sex be harmful at my age – will it damage my health?

I'm a bit embarrassed to mention it, but when my fiance kisses and fondles me I do feel an excited response, although he doesn't realise it. I am certainly aware of his excitement. I feel very shy at the thought of our wedding night but I love him and I hope you're not going to say there's no fool like an old fool. Thanks, Marje.

Says Marje

What I'm going to say is, there's no fool like a young fool who thinks that sex was invented by and exclusively for youth. What they don't realise, poor little darlings, is that they too will one day be collecting their bus passes if they're lucky enough to live that long. And I hope they'll have the same positive, healthy attitude to life and love that you've got.

And talking about health, sex won't harm you. On the contrary, it'll do you a power of good. It's obvious that your active hormones are still leaping out, hence that surge of excited response when your boyfriend starts snogging.

From your shy investigations of his still lively anatomy, you can look forward to many nights of love.

The fact that he's been married before is a plus. He'll know what to do.

He's done it all before, though I take the view that with each new relationship there's a wonderful feeling of complete renewal so that it will probably seem to him, as it will be to you, the very first time.

Age has little to do with sexual pleasure, though sometimes enjoyment can be increased for a bus pass lady by the use of a lubricating cream or gel which you can get from the chemist.

Your new husband will take longer to get aroused and stay aroused than he once did but one of the advantages of age, for both of you, is that the longer it takes the nicer it is.

I'm sure he'll give you guidance about what to do. If in doubt, ask him for it. No need to be shy.

He'll be your husband, dammit, the person closest to you in the world, the friend and companion and lover who'll change you from a nervous woman to a confident wife.

It's never too late to find happiness, as you have discovered. And here's hoping you both enjoy it forever.

He fears his urge is too little, too late

Dear Marje

My bride-to-be left me at the church – literally – classic jilt, with all the guests and me waiting. That was 23 years ago and the effect was devastating.

I became impotent and unable to make new relationships. As the years went by, my sex-drive gradually came back but I was afraid to see women friends and for a time I used prostitutes and felt horrible and disgusting. Eventually I

settled into a rut, dispirited and self-pitying. Then the miracle occurred.

I met a wonderful woman who, at 43, is four years my junior. She knows my history. She understands my sexual needs and the occasional bouts of impotence I get.

We are going to be married and we long for a family. We've had medical checks, and we are fit.

We know the risks but do you think we're too old to give children a good life or if we'll be too decrepit when it really matters?

Says Marje

Bear with me while I do my sums. You are now 47, right? And you were 24 when your bride changed her mind at the last minute. Although you appear to have fixed the blame for all your subsequent problems on her, I wonder why she ditched you so dramatically. Have you ever considered that even all those years ago your sex drive could have been less than powerful? Did the girl who jilted you perhaps fear that life with you could have been a life of sexual frustration?

The reason I ask is because I feel that the understandably bitter grudge you've carried for so long against her may have more to do with your in-built sexual difficulties than the loss of the girl herself.

The new lady is, indeed, the miracle you needed to help you to sort yourself out. And having children by someone you love would complete your rehabilitation.

But although there seems to be no physical barrier, is there a danger that you want to be a father for the wrong reasons? Do you want children as symbols of your return, whole again, to the human race?

I realise I'm asking you questions instead of answering the one you put to me. But I think you ought to be absolutely clear about your motives before embarking on fatherhood.

I don't consider either of you too old to cope with kids though when they arrive you'll probably both yearn for the peace you have right now. But that can be said of parents at whatever age they start their families.

In idealising children, there's a very big danger of losing sight of their noisy, rumbustious reality.

If you regard them like the romantic decorations on your

wedding cake, forget about having them. And settle down happily for the future with the woman who will surely help you wipe out the misery of the past.

Stumped by an age-old question

Dear Marje

Five years ago, aged 28, I fell for a gorgeous hunk seven years younger. We moved in together, and ever since I've wanted us to get married.

He's not bothered and says married or not makes no difference to the way we feel. I've nagged him a bit and made a couple of scenes, but he's really good-tempered.

So I was amazed when a couple of weeks ago, he gave me an engagement ring, and said: "Right, choose the date." He then kept me awake nearly all night making love and said we would go to Egypt for our honeymoon.

But when we met I told him I was the same age as him. I'm faced now with revealing the truth for the marriage certificate and getting a passport. I've never been abroad before. I know he loves me but how will he react? What excuse can I make to get out of this stupid mess I've made of my life?

Says Marje

It's a stupid situation, for sure. But steady on. It isn't a major tragedy and it won't spoil your life if you handle it carefully.

Your loved one sounds like the stuff a woman's dreams are made of. Hunky, amiable, romantic and enthusiastic when the occasion demands and very sensitive to the way you feel about marriage. Or maybe he'd rather brace himself and go through with it than face further scenes and a lifetime of nagging.

It's to be hoped his sense of humour prevails when you tell him the truth. As you should. You could hedge and say you'd changed your mind about getting wed, that you're sure Eastbourne is much more stylish than Egypt, but why go on living such a foolish lie? Explain you fibbed because you didn't want to lose him and that you were scared he'd drop you if he'd known the truth. And that, of course, is the truth and if he loves you as much as it seems, he'll laugh it off and spend another night convincing you it's of no consequence.

You demonstrate symptoms of insecurity. Your longing to be tied by marriage vows and the lie about your age are classic signs.

I think your lover is aware of this insecurity and it's his love for you and concern for you that prompted him to buy the ring. The nagging and scenes would have driven away a man who loved you less. I don't think his love will be shaken when you confess your foolish little white lie. He'll understand perfectly the anxiety that prompted it.

P.S. Another wife aged 45, who is also in the age fib game, has put a false date on her marriage certificate. She asks me to tell her if she has committed a crime.

My pet legal eagle says that yes, it is an offence to give a false statement, but it's most unlikely that she'd receive anything more than a rap on the knuckles and a fine.

Haunted by a honeymoon confession

Dear Marje

Before our wedding six months ago, my wife and I enjoyed a very good sex life. But on our honeymoon the story my wife told me horrified me and has threatened our relationship.

It appears that her grandfather abused her sexually until he died when she was eight years old.

She said she adored him and had no idea that what he did was wrong. She never told her parents. In fact, she'd carried the secret until she told me. She had a great childhood with loving parents.

We are very happy except for one thing which is making me extremely uneasy. When we have sex, she wants me to hurt her. The other night she asked me to hit her.

I am not vicious. I can't bear to hurt anyone and the effect of all this is to turn me off. Could the business with

34

Says Marje

Without doubt, her grandfather's appalling treatment is why your wife wants you to abuse her now.

Because she loved him so much she saw no evil in what he did to her. It was, for her, a demonstration of his love.

And now that she loves you, she wants what she only remembers as a happy time to continue. Your wife makes perverted demands on you because a pervert taught her. She trusted and loved him as now she trust and loves you.

It's a tragedy that she kept her secret to herself for so long. Victims of abuse can be helped if only they can bring themselves to talk about their experiences. One big plus for you is that your wife has been able to talk frankly to you.

This will help you to help her and could save your marriage, threatened from the moment she asked you to inflict pain on her. You are not a sadist who would get a sexual buzz doing it.

For you it's a turn-off and if you are unable to get an erection because of your wife's demands, the marriage doesn't stand much chance of survival.

You must begin by explaining that you cannot hurt and punish her, however much she begs you to. And you need to impress on her the vital importance of seeking counselling.

I'm sure she doesn't realise she needs it and you've got the tricky job of convincing her that she does. She may deny that her sexual demands are perverted. I suggest you contact The British Association for Counselling. Send an SAE to: 1 Regent Place, Rugby, CV21 2PJ. Or phone 0788 578328. They should be able to arrange for counselling.

Get a move on before the sins of the grandparent destroy the life of the girl who loved him much more than he deserved.

Will ex ruin the wedding day?

Dear Marje

We are all very excited, preparing for my only daughter's wedding. Apart from the usual good-natured arguments about the catering and who should be invited, there are no

real problems. I should be the happiest bride's mother on earth. But there's one snag.

I myself got married a month ago. I am divorced from my first husband, the bride's father. I'd like to say we are still friends but I detest him. He seriously abused me and is a very heavy drinker but he does idolise our girl.

He is a generous father, I'll give him that. He is paying for the wedding and has given her money towards their home. But he treats me like I'm a bad smell and has been very rude to my new husband.

I am worried about what will happen on the wedding day. Naturally I'll be with my husband. My ex will be alone and there could be a punch-up, knowing him. My daughter will want both her parents close to her. Is there any way round this problem?

Says Marje

Although a wedding is a great day for the young couple's parents, no one should forget that the most important people present are the bride and groom. They are the leading players.

The rest, such as yourself, merely have supporting roles. And while it's important that you have a happy day, it's a thousand times more important that your daughter's day is one she'll remember and treasure all her life.

Wouldn't it be awful if, because you couldn't prevent your loathing for her father showing through your clenched teeth, the punch-up you dread occurred? A muttered insult from you or a nasty sneer from him and your daughter's day could end in disaster.

I daresay that since he's footing what sounds like quite a bill, the bride's dad will be strutting his stuff and after several toasts to the health of the bride and groom, he'll probably demonstrate the aggressive tendencies you grew to hate.

I think that if you go prepared for the worst, with luck and good sense, it won't happen. Paint a sweet smile on your face as you put on your lipstick and your new hat to get ready for the ceremony.

Presumably her father will give the bride away. You should fade as far into the background, without actually crouching behind a pew, as possible. School your husband, too, to be part of the scenery. Do not put yourself forward and keep as far away from danger, i.e. your ex, as you can.

It won't be easy for the proud mother of the bride to play such a low-key role but I think it's the only way to ensure the occasion is a happy one for your girl.

You can, I'm sure, rely on your new husband for the support you'll need to console you for what could have been a happier wedding day for your daughter if only her parents had had a happier marriage.

Groomed for a lie

Dear Marje

My girlfriend and I started dating when she was 17 and, because her parents were very strict, we told them I was only two years older. In fact I was 25.

We've been going steady now for three years and are planning our wedding. We are both very worried because obviously her mother and father will now have to be told the truth about my age. She's terrified they will stop us getting married. Can they do this?

She thinks her mother might be on her side but she is scared of her father who is very dictatorial and there's not much love lost between him and me anyway.

I am sure he's jealous because his darling daughter loves me. Our wedding is next month. Can you please advise us what to do?

Says Marje

I'm puzzled about why you imagined that knocking six years off your age would make you more acceptable to your girlfriend's parents than if they knew you were a few years older.

It was a foolish mistake and I'm not going to kid you that a confession now will mean her mother and father will give you a warm embrace and cry "welcome to the family, son".

They won't. They'll probably mark you down as a deceitful git. Or her father will, because he'll be only too glad to have a good reason for giving you a kick in the rear. Now he'll have a good reason why he shouldn't trust you. Can they, you ask, stop you getting married? No, your girlfriend is over 18.

But they can refuse to take part in the wedding. And you will have a very unhappy bride on your hands if she is forced to split with her family. But since she was party to the plot to deceive them, she shares the responsibility of telling them the truth.

Her parents are by no means guilt-free. If she was so intimidated by them that she couldn't bring herself to mention her boyfriend was eight years her senior, they can't be high in the good parent league.

But since no one's perfect, neither you nor them, here's hoping you can all be indulgent towards each other's faults. Perhaps you will be able to convince them that 28 is not middle-aged. I hope they count themselves lucky you're not 58.

But after the honeymoon, I urge you most strongly to make friends with your in-laws. Remember, family life begins when the wedding is only a memory.

Why won't her son flee his torturer?

Dear Marje

This is to remind you and everyone else that not all battered wives are innocent victims of brutal men.

My son's wife is very vicious, with a lashing tongue, bitter spite and frequent physical attacks on him.

She's attacked him in his bed with a broom and a knife. She'll use any weapon that comes to hand. I even fear for his life.

And when my son finally loses his rag and hits her and she gets the police, what do they find? A small, tearful, shaking little woman who seems bewildered at what's been done to her. Is it surprising she drives my son mad?

Thank God the police soon size up the situation and my son has never been charged. Isn't it time women like my daughter-in-law were exposed for the sake of men like my son?

Says Marje

I am more than willing to denounce your vicious daughter-in-law and other women like her. Just as I denounce brutal and vicious men. As far as I know, the proportion of women like your son's wife is very small compared to the large number of violent men.

I would never deny that women are as equally skilled in the business of cruelty as men. But generally, a woman uses her tongue as her deadly weapon.

And as your son has discovered, a woman's spiteful tongue can send a normally amiable man into raging overdrive and goad him into using a man's extremely effective weapon, his knuckle. Your letter gives no hint as to why your son's wife is so horrendous to him. Clearly, you are in a fine old rage yourself right now, but do you really know enough about their marriage to judge it? It may have started out like it was made in heaven, but why is it now apparently such hell? And here is another question for you. Why does your son continue to live with this virago? It's usually a lot easier for a man to leave a woman than it is for a woman to walk out on a man. I'm sure he knows you'd gladly offer him bed and board.

So doesn't it strike you as odd that he puts up with it? It does me.

There is a psychological condition known as sado-masochism, meaning that one partner gets a huge buzz out of being cruel and the other out of being the willing victim. Many sado-masochistic partnerships flourish happily.

There's a very strong sexual element in this kind of relationship, though sometimes it gets out of hand and the victim would give anything to escape.

Your son, if he wants to, could escape his torture. Perhaps it's never occurred to such a loving and concerned mother that the truth is he simply doesn't want to.

No escape from this evil in-law

Dear Marje

My mother-in-law is a rotten old woman. Ever since I married her son she has pulled the emotional blackmail strings, and believe me, she's a mistress of it.

We can't escape from her. Even on holiday her calls and letters haunt us, reducing my husband to a guilt-ridden wreck. She complains about everything, that we're not visiting her enough/giving her enough money/letting her see enough of the children.

If I had my way she'd never see them again. She is a really nasty piece of work and I don't want her to influence them.

Even her friends find her awful, though the way she talks about them, it's amazing she's got any.

I wish I knew why she was so hateful. I long to bash her. I can't of course, because of my husband – so he and I fight instead.

She is destroying my life and I need advice, please, about how to cope with her.

I think you need advice about coping with yourself, actually. Your mother-in-law is a fact of life.

You married her son for better or worse, and she comes under the heading of worse.

And though I'll grant you she sounds like a very severe pain in the nether regions, there is no way you are going to remove her from your life.

One of the tough aspects of marriage is that you marry your loved one's family too.

I have no way of knowing why your ma-in-law is a rotten old woman, I only know that one day, if you're lucky enough to live that long, you'll be an old woman, too. By which time, hopefully, you'll have learned to be tolerant and to accept the undeniable fact that while people can choose their friends, they can't choose their relatives.

Your husband, it seems, defends his mother from your tart tongue. Clearly, he doesn't share your view that she's evil.

It might get you somewhere to give calm thought to her complaints.

Are you, in fact, keeping the kids away from her the way a lot of mean daughters-in-law do, just to get your own back? Have you been dodging visiting her out of spite?

I can't comment on the money issue. But if she depends on her son for a top-up to her old age pension, and if it's given grudgingly, no wonder she bears a grudge.

There are always two sides to the in-law battle and in the end, neither side wins, and the man in the middle is the loser.

I don't ask you to love this nasty piece of work, but for goodness sake, calm down and get your priorities in order before you allow one silly and probably lonely old lady to wreck your life and marriage. Remember, as the wife you enjoy pole position – though there's no need to rub it in to her.

Mother's pride gets the boot

Dear Marje

On her wedding day my daughter-in-law told me how lucky she was to have met my son. And she was, too. She got her hands on all his money, she had a nice house and the love of a good man.

Ten years later she seems determined to throw it all away and to hurt my son as much as possible in the process. Last month she threw him and all his belongings out of the house. This week she has moved herself and the three children to a women's refuge.

I can't believe she's got the gall to let people believe he would harm her. He's never laid a finger on her and he idolises his children. But because there's going to be a court case she won't let him visit them.

I hate to see him suffering like this. And do his children have to suffer too? Is there any way his desperate mother can help him?

Says Marje

Desperate you may well be, but you are also blinkered, blind to your son's faults and weaknesses. That's only natural, but before you condemn his wife out of hand, ask yourself how you can be so sure your son has never been violent.

Women do not lug their children off to a women's refuge out of some foolish whim. These refuges may be safe places, but they are not luxury hotels with all mod-cons.

No woman would voluntarily run to such a refuge unless she was desperate and frightened – especially one like your daughter-in-law, who you say, has a nice home.

A nice home can be a torture chamber if the man of the house is violent. You claim he wouldn't have laid a finger on her, but you would wouldn't you? He was never going to pop round to visit his mum and say "I beat her up again last night, the spiteful cow".

I'm not going to suggest either, that his wife might be a blameless angel. She could, indeed, be a spiteful cow. You imply that she is.

Like so many prejudiced mothers-in-law, you can't see any good in her and I don't suppose she's all that gone on you either. But however much a wife may goad her husband, violent behaviour is totally unacceptable.

My great regret in all this is that your son's frightened wife doesn't appear to have anyone to turn to who cares about her and the children. I can't comment on the forthcoming court case. I only know that the best interests of the children will be the court's priority.

But it would be in the best interest of your family life, and a future relationship with your grandchildren, if only you could accept that your son is not the saint you've pretended he is – only mortal and flawed like most of us.

Could you ever bring yourself to offer to help his wife? No, I didn't really think so. Pity.

Forbidden passion is a cruel joke

Dear Marje

I am a man with a mother-in-law problem. But it's not the usual interfering old-bitch-type situation. On the contrary. She is a 55-year-old stunner.

When I married her daughter 12 years ago, my best man said: "If she turns out to be a looker like her mum when she's her age, you're in luck."

Well, my wife is more like her chubby, boot-faced dad.

I admit I have fancied my mother-in-law for years but I repressed my feelings because I really do love my good-natured, good-humoured wife, and I've never been unfaithful to her until a few weeks ago when I went to her mother's flat to fix some fuses. We had a few drinks too many and that's when it began.

We are having a passionate affair and both of us feel guilty as hell, but it's like a drug habit we can't break. It would kill my wife if she found out.

What I'm asking you is, how do I kick this drug that's nearly killing me?

Says Marje

Dependence on any drug, whether it's one like Ecstasy or the sort of ecstasy you are experiencing with your mother-in-law, is very hard indeed to conquer.

But the main difference between the drug you're addicted to and the one airheaded kids buy from evil pushers is that

43

Ecstasy with a capital E usually damages only the one hooked on it. Your drug could destroy the lives of three people. At least, I imagine there must be other members of the family who would be totally devastated if this affair was revealed.

Your chubby, boot-faced father-in-law, for one. You don't mention children. Imagine the effect it would have on them. Sex is, indeed, an immensely powerful and effective drug and I'm not about to say to you use your will-power, man, and simply walk away and never go near the woman again, even if every light in her flat fuses. Let chubby-chops mend the fuses.

But only if both you and your passionate ma-in-law can face up to the reality of this affair and where it could lead will you be able to sort this problem out.

I can't sort it out for you. I can only spell out the disaster ahead if you can't end the affair.

The sad thing about relationships based solely on sexual gratification and the buzz that an illicit affair brings is that unless there's something more to it than sex – like love and friendship too – the sex element inevitably wanes.

Most men begin waning in their mid-twenties, though few realise it and many manage to struggle on into ripe old age. You probably imagine your passion will never wane.

Believe me, it will. Or hers will.

And what'll be left? Two guilty, unhappy people who'll wonder if it was worth all the pain and the sacrifice.

No one can make the choice or the decision to kick the drug but yourself.

And believe me, I know how tough the choice will be when, as I think you will, you kick it.

Ma-in-law is such a bitter pill

Dear Marje

My 19-year-old daughter has a mother-in-law problem, even before her wedding.

Her boyfriend's mother is a successful businesswoman, one of those power-dressed, bossy types who always knows best about everything.

She organised the buying of their home, the furnishings and even chose the wallpaper. The latest outrage is she's asked my daughter what contraception they'll use and told her she should go on the Pill. As my girl and her boyfriend have been together for two years and often stay with us and share her bedroom, I'm sure they know all about contraception. But as the wedding-day gets close, my daughter is getting very nervous and edgy. I'm sure this awful, bossy woman is the main cause.

What can I do to help my daughter to cope with her? Her boyfriend, who takes after his father, is easy-going and not the sort to stand up to her.

Says Marje

There are very few young brides who are lucky enough not to have to cope with a mother-in-law problem. One small advantage your girl has over many is that at least she knows what she's got to deal with.

If she's sensible and can keep her temper under control, a young wife can smile blandly and say, "Yes, Mum, how right you are" to every interfering suggestion and to the pressures over-possessive mothers put on their sons' wives.

It's not easy, for the temptation is to tell the woman to bog off, but your daughter sounds too well-brought-up to come out with such a rough response. And far too timid. It's plain that her power-suited tormentor intimidates her.

It's a pity her son is like his dad, a bit wimpish. The father is almost certainly henpecked to a degree where he's given up trying to assert himself and I hope he's a member of a nice golf club or escapes somehow from his organisation-mad wife. The mistake your daughter made was allowing this woman to take charge in the first place.

But because she's got a wise mum, she will know how to listen to her mother-in-law's instructions and quietly do her own thing. I'm not in favour of confrontation in a situation like this. It can result in a divided family and never-ending warfare.

Of course, it was outrageous of her future mother-in-law to muscle in on the couple's family planning, but I'd give her the benefit of the doubt on this one. She could have meant it kindly, and plainly she's unaware that they've been at it now for ages. She doesn't need to know, either.

The best advice you can give your daughter is to remind her that when you marry, you acquire a family, whether or not you

45

like or loathe them. And you've simply got to shrug and put up with them as cheerfully and as tactfully as you can.

Outcast by her mother-in-law

Dear Marje

I am having real trouble with my mother-in-law. She isn't actually my mother-in-law because her son and I aren't married. We started living together about two years ago and we have a baby daughter. His mother was nasty to me from the start but when the baby was born she was foul. You'd think I was a hooker.

Sometimes we ask her to babysit but she always refuses. Yet she's nice to his brother's wife and often babysits for them. She pointedly refuses to talk to me and she doesn't want to hold the baby.

Her husband is quite different, very kind and he is very happy to cuddle his grandchild. I have always done by best to get on with her for my boyfriend's sake because naturally he loves his mother.

But he knows she makes me unhappy and this gets him down. I don't want him to be torn between us. Can you help me to improve our relationship?

Says Marje

You put your finger on the root of the problem when you said this spiteful woman treats you like a hooker. That's the way she sees you.

You live with a man you are not married to and this makes you, in her eyes, no better than a prostitute. It's escaped her notice that countless couples today live together without feeling the need to seal their love with a legal bit of paper.

She is old-fashioned. She thinks you are immoral and I daresay it enrages her to have to accept your illegitimate offspring as her grand-daughter.

The mother-in-law, daughter-in-law relationship is usually pretty fraught. A man's mother resents the girl he loves and believes she has stolen him away from the mother who feels she has first claim.

And in your situation, its far, far worse, for she's convinced that not only have you stolen him, but that you have the gall to live with him in what she regards as an immoral union.

You can see, can't you, why she looks on you as an enemy? Then there are also the neighbours. What must they think, she asks herself. She reckons the 'scandal' rubs off on her.

I'm sure she puts all the blame on you, despite her son being your fully consenting partner. Her other son is 'respectably' married, so his wife is OK.

She gets the approval and help which you are denied. I guess its the price you have to pay for being unconventional by her standards. Perhaps you can now see her motives and can understand why she's so nasty.

I'm afraid you will either have to shrug and bear it, or get married. But it would be a big mistake to do that simply to pacify this woman. I doubt if she'll ever change.

Take comfort in her husband's affection. He sounds nice enough to make up for her meanness.

Busybody mum wrecks marriage

Dear Marje

When my son married, his wife became the daughter I never had. We were very close.

The marriage was very happy and they have two daughters, wonderful for me. I babysat and had the children whenever their parents went out.

Then my son and his wife ran into a bad patch. She started going out a lot with her girlfriends and he didn't like it.

I talked them into going for counselling but it didn't do much good. I told my son to let his wife have a bit of freedom and I'd have the children. He took my advice but she met up with some man, a bad lot, and now they've parted and she has turned against me.

She won't come to my home and won't let me see the children. Because I miss them so much, I rang her, but she hung up on me.

My son, who is trying to get her back, says it's all my fault for interfering. How ungrateful can your children be? Is it any wonder I am depressed?

Says Marje

I agree with your son. You appear to have tried to direct his life and marriage from the moment you set eyes on the girl.

It's easy enough to understand why you so desperately wanted the marriage to work. It wasn't just because your son's happiness was important, it was because you wanted to smother his wife with mother-love. And smother you did.

It's a pity there was no-one around to warn you that the offer of well-meaning advice could be taken as interference.

When the counselling failed they probably blamed you. I can hear your daughter-in-law muttering "why doesn't the interfering old bat mind her own business?"

I daresay your son blamed you when she went out with friends and met up with that bad lot. None of it was your fault. But probably what gets your daughter-in-law's goat is your possessiveness towards your grandchildren. You did your best to make a takeover bid and she bitterly resents this. There is often trouble in a family when gran gets closer and closer to the children and mum gets more and more resentful.

It happens a lot, when working mums have to rely on grans for babysitting. For the mums, the gratitude is often mixed with jealously. Tact and give and take is needed by both sides.

Perhaps, after a couple of weeks, you could write to your daughter-in-law, saying you are genuinely sorry, that all you wanted was their happiness and if you sometimes put your foot in it, you didn't mean any harm.

Emphasise how much you miss her – don't mention the children. You can do no more and I hope one day you'll be a united, happy family.

She can't forgive his years of cheating

Dear Marje

My daughter and her husband have got themselves into a ridiculous situation and, though I could happily bang their heads together, I feel I've got to help them.

My son-in-law came home a few weeks ago and confessed

he'd been having an affair with a girl in his office. That was bad enough, but when he told my daughter it had started three weeks after they married and lasted until three months ago, she threw him out and she's changed the locks of the house and says she will divorce him.

They've been married for 11 years and they've always been so happy. Surely she could forgive, if not forget.

He has told me he loves my daughter and bitterly regrets the affair which, he says, he couldn't stop because the girl was blackmailing him and threatening to tell his wife. That's why he finally confessed.

My daughter says that as far as she's concerned he no longer exists. What can I do to patch things up for them?

Says Marje

Not a thing, I'm afraid. All you can do is hope they'll sort themselves out. But don't be too optimistic and don't imagine that your advice to your daughter will be acceptable.

You are asking a lot of her. Your son-in-law has been sleeping with this girl at work for the best part of 11 years and presumably he's been having his conjugals in the matrimonial bed, too.

It's reasonable to hope a wife could manage to overlook a casual, brief dalliance. Or a drunken one-night stand. If a woman can make an excuse for a man she loves and wants to hang on to, she will.

She'll blame pressure on him at work, or his being led astray by boozy colleagues, or even kid herself some sleazy bimbo seduced him. And she'll forgive him just this once and it had better not happen again. Or else.

But your daughter has been betrayed consistently over years. The girl is his long-time mistress.

I think the blackmail threat was probably a load of eye-wash. Why should this female start putting the frighteners on him now, after all this time? The more likely explanation is that she was pressurising him to leave your daughter to marry her. Maybe he figured the only way to get her off his back was to confess.

I doubt if it ever dawned on him that his patient wife would tell him to get stuffed. I hope she won't relent, for there can be life after divorce and it would be great for her to find a man who would value her and be faithful. There are still a few of this dying breed around. But if you did manage to get her back with her husband again, I'm sure she'd end up forever suspicious, bitter and soured.

You want better for her than that. Which is why I suggest you button your lip, except to mention that whatever she decides, you are on her side, supporting her through what's going to be a painful experience.

So cool about a nappy event

Dear Marje

I am 37 and pregnant with our first child after seven years of trying. We are both over the moon. There's only one tiny fly in the ointment. My husband's parents are elderly and very stiff and formal.

I have a rather cool relationship with them and they pinched their mouths a bit when we told them our news. My mother-in-law remarked I was rather old to be starting a family.

She is already laying down the law about when I should stop working and assuming I won't go back to my job. The other evening I was wearing tight leggings and a T-shirt and she said it was a disgusting way to dress, that I should wear a proper maternity frock to conceal my condition.

I'm afraid I took out my rage on my poor husband that night and refused him conjugal rights. He has offered to talk to his mother but says it would be more sensible to say nothing and keep the peace. I hope you'll understand my outrage.

Says Marje

I do, I do. Only too well do I understand it. And I reckon you are very wise to grasp this particular nettle early on in the game – if your spouse will forgive me for calling his dear mother a nettle. She is prickly enough to rate the label.

I feel rather sorry for her son. This situation could be building up to a head-on collision between the two women in his life. Both are already setting up the goal posts. And you

50

were foolish enough to score an own goal by rejecting him in bed as a punishment, silly woman. Don't ever do that again.

You realise, don't you, that her scathing remarks about your appearance have nothing whatever to do with the pregnant bulge the T-shirt displayed? She is simply using it as an excuse to get at you, the way so many jealous mothers-in-law get at the women their beloved sons marry.

She, in fact, is far more foolish than you are. She could be the loser in this game of not-very-happy families. Her son won't want to take sides but she might force him to.

She could end up as one of the very large army of grandparents deprived of the pleasure of their children's children.

You'd do well to listen to your husband's advice. Go on smiling sweetly, however snide the remarks, and plan your life the way you both want it.

I foresee your relationship with your in-laws will always be touchy. But you can do a lot towards keeping it reasonably calm, simply by pretending that it is. It's never easy, the in-law relationship.

But it can take a miraculous turn for the better with the announcement of the birth. It would be tragic if you let Mrs Prickle mar your good fortune.

A better life beckons with a brother-in-law

Dear Marje

I am hopelessly in love with my husband's brother and he says he loves me. We have made love a few times though he's not as passionate as my husband.

I married very young. My then boyfriend had made me pregnant but he refused to marry me just because I was expecting and I was very hurt about that. My twins were nearly two before he agreed to the wedding.

He is an aggressive and argumentative bully and he's also very secretive. The only thing that has kept us together is sex.

It's the best part of our relationship and he makes sure I

51

have plenty of orgasms. Sex apart, we are totally incompatible.

Now I have to decide whether to move in with his brother. Please don't write to me at home. I don't want to hurt my husband who, if he found your letter, would discover how much I love his younger brother.

Says Marje

It's difficult to understand why you are so reluctant to hurt your husband when it seems he's been hurting you for years.

It's a bit of luck you've got such a good sex life. Apparently you have little else.

But it sounds like you wouldn't even have good sex with his brother, who in addition to being boring in bed might turn out to have your husband's unpleasant characteristics as well. They share the same genes, after all.

I'm not too keen on a man who seems to feel no compunction about sleeping with his brother's wife. It's interesting that you say you are "hopelessly" in love with him

The hopeless bit indicates that the whole thing is a fantasy you've invented to escape from the reality of your unsatisfactory marriage.

You dream of a happy-ever-after life with your brother-in-law, knowing perfectly well you'll never leave your husband.

In your fantasies you probably imagine that while your husband is providing you with all those orgasms you are in his brother's arms.

If you were crazy enough to move in with your brother-in-law you'd be facing countless new problems including family problems.

There'd certainly be trouble with the parents-in-law. Then there are the twins. Do you expect them to regard their uncle as a new daddy?

The time has come to stop dreaming and make an effort to bring reality into your life.

Like talking straight to your husband and reminding him and yourself that there's a lot of room for improvement if the marriage is to survive.

Maybe in the end it won't but it's worth a try. Just give your brother-in-law a sisterly kiss and say goodbye to a relationship that can only add up to danger.

TEMPTATIONS and INFIDELITIES

Can three-in-a-bed save this marriage?

Dear Marje

I had suspected for some time that my husband was seeing another woman.

I found condoms under some of his shirts and I'm on the Pill. That was the first clue. There were others. The usual "working late at the office", suddenly weekend "business" conferences and so on. I decided to confront him and he confessed.

He met her at work. At 26 she's 10 years younger than I am. Unlike me, she has no children. I have three young daughters. She lives in a bed-sit where he visits her for sex. He was amazingly frank about it.

He says she satisfies his sexual needs which I know nothing about. Perverted practices, probably.

He swears he loves me and doesn't want this affair to break up our marriage but he's made an incredible suggestion which, he says, will preserve it.

He wants the girl to occupy our spare room. At first I shouted "no way". But now I'm having second thoughts. I'll do anything to keep him, even share him. What do you think of his idea?

Says Marje

Not a lot, actually. Not, at any rate, from your point of view. I can see why it would be great for your husband and his mistress. He would no longer need to sneak off into what is probably the grotty bed-sit where she lives.

He could enjoy all home comforts without any inconvenience. Presumably, since you and he still have the conjugals, he'd service the two of you. popping into her room when he felt like engaging in those mysterious practices.

The implication is you've denied him these "pleasures". A woman has an absolute right to reject practices that revolt or

53

offend her. But as you've discovered, there's no shortage of other women who'll oblige.

If you decide to agree to this bizarre arrangement, there are several aspects to consider. He may suggest three-in-a-bed to save himself the trouble of moving from room to room. Would you be willing to co-operate?

Then there are the household practicalities. As they dash off to work in the mornings, will you be doing her room? Putting her washing in the machine? Will she eat with the family? I can picture the cosy threesome sharing the steak and kidney pud you've made.

Then there are the children. It'll seem very puzzling indeed to them. They'll soon get wise to the fact that she's no ordinary lodger.

It can't possibly work. And if this plan is your husband's idea of a solution to your marriage problems, he's the number one cuckoo in cloud cuckoo land. He takes first prize for unmitigated cheek.

If hanging on to this girl is the price he demands for preserving your marriage, it simply isn't worth preserving.

Some women could go along with such a scheme. I do not believe you could and I think your husband should be told to make a choice. You'd have to take the chance that he might choose her.

Secret sex danger on the school run

Dear Marje

As an out of work dad, with a wife still in a job, I agreed to do all the chores including taking the kids to school. When I was working my wife did the school run.

We've had problems in our marriage recently. I'm depressed and our sex life has suffered and I have bouts of impotence and my wife is irritable and sharp-tempered.

There's one consolation in my life. It is one of the mothers I meet at the school gates. She's no glamour girl but she's marvellously cheerful. She is also very sympathetic and even encourages me to moan!

We started sitting together to chat in the car after we'd

54

dropped our children off but now we drive to a quiet spot and we've been petting and fondling each other and I see danger ahead.

She's divorced and she's got nothing to lose. But there are risks for me. When I'm with her, I get strong erections all the time. You can see my dilemma, I'm sure. The question is should I or shouldn't I? What would be your advice?

Says Marje

I'm not quite sure from your vague question what you're asking advice about.

Should you or shouldn't you stop all the messing about in the car? Or should you get on and do the job properly and make the school run a real pleasure? Or perhaps the question is a more serious one? Is there a future for you with this agreeable lady whose caresses arouse you to the level of passion missing from your marriage?

I think you are afraid to face any of these questions, which is why you posed them so vaguely.

But you will have to face them. You must seem like a gift from heaven to this lone woman. She's probably even more sexually frustrated than you are. After all, you do have sex on and off with your wife.

Incidentally, the occasional impotence isn't unusual.

Most men experience it at some time in their active sex lives, usually when there's a particular stress, like being out of work.

You wife's ill-humour could be because she, too, is hungry for sex and because she's also having to carry the extra burden of being the sole breadwinner.

You've put me in the difficult position of trying to answer a question you haven't asked.

But if your cuddling sessions in the car continue, I doubt if you'll be able to stay zipped up for much longer.

And because relationships rarely stand still, things will move fast and you'll both be in love and then there will be the even more serious question, like do you leave your wife to set up home with this other woman?

You've arrived at the point when you know you must make a decision, but you are the only one, I'm afraid, who can make it. But I hope you remember when the moment of truth arrives that while your friend has nothing to lose, you have plenty.

Flushed with jealousy

Dear Marje

From the start, I was determined not to be a jealous wife. My husband was – and still is – every woman's dream. Tall, athletic and very good-looking.

I could understand why women were after him and he, of course, basked in the attention. He flirted with them all.

What I couldn't understand was why he chose to marry plain, ordinary me. But I know he loved me. He was 25 when we got married. Now he's 52 and, as he grows older, he's making passes at younger and younger girls.

At a party recently, he spent the whole evening slobbering over a long-legged bimbo aged about 19 and she was obviously loving it. After that party, I had it out with him and told him I couldn't take any more of it. He laughed and said I must be menopausal and why didn't I get something for my hot flushes.

Tell me, Marje, why is it men are so cruel and thoughtless? I said did he want to leave me and he laughed again, gave me a kiss and told me to be my age.

Says Marje

I am not as bothered about your flirtatious spouse as I am about you. Here you are, married for 27 years to this conceited dreamboat, yet you still denigrate and underestimate yourself.

Can't you see how lucky your husband is to be married to you? And can't you understand that he knows it?

To him, these bimbos are a bit of harmless fun. Their eager response to his flirtatious behaviour reinforces his self-image. You make him sound like a sort of Richard Gere knocking on a bit. He's always had this starry image of himself and for years you, along with all the bimbos, have helped to keep it going and it's no bad thing.

It has kept him happy and kept you happy, too, it seems. Until now. Those cracks of his about you being flushed and menopausal were clearly the sort of banter fond married couples exchange. But I suspect he unknowingly put his finger on your problem.

It's not a sudden rush of jealousy to the head of a woman who has, for years, understood why other women are knocked out by her old man. It's a realisation, I think, that age is beginning to catch up on you, as it is on him. But he's never going to let it bother him.

You, though, because you have a very poor self-image will let it bother you. Why is your view of yourself such a poor one? That dishy man could, it seems have had any woman he wanted. He wanted you above all others. He still does.

He laughs at your anger because he knows there's no reason for it. He wouldn't swap you for any long-legged bimbo. He loves you. He jokes with you, not to be cruel, but to make you feel better. He may be a bit insensitive but he knows how lucky he is.

It would do no harm though, to check up on those flushes. He may have stumbled on a point there.

Haunted by her sex fling

Dear Marje

I am desperate to confess a guilty secret that has haunted me for nearly 10 years.

My marriage was going through a sticky period. My husband was predictable and selfish sexually, always taking it for granted that whenever he wanted it, I had to be ready for it though often I wasn't.

I suppose I was ripe for an affair and a man at work was keen and I had fun for a few months. Then I came to my senses. The man and I didn't love one another and I felt cheap and we finished.

But the affair made me realise how important my husband was to me and how stupid I'd been.

I got him to discuss our problems and although things didn't change right away, gradually everything got better.

I was worried about HIV and other sexually transmitted diseases because I knew the man was promiscuous and I went for tests. They were negative but I still worry. I also carry a great load of guilt and although I'm sure my husband would leave me if he knew, I am terribly tempted to tell him. Do you think it would help me if I did?

Says Marje

No, I do not. It would help neither you nor your husband. You are convinced such a confession would destroy your marriage and I think it almost certainly would.

Even if your husband was able to forgive and forget your infidelity, the rest of your married life would be blighted.

Trust would vanish. Sex would probably revert to the old pattern. He'd use it to punish rather than please you. You say he was selfish before you had the important heart-to-heart that restored your marriage.

Don't you see how selfish it would be of you to destroy his peace of mind, simply to assuage your guilt?

It is the guilt that's behind your longing to confess. The huge relief of confession would certainly make you feel better but haven't you considered what it could do to him?

It would immensely damage his self-esteem to learn you had a lover with whom you enjoyed good sex while sex with your husband wasn't good enough.

I think guilt, too, is the reason for your continuing anxiety about your health. You can be absolutely confident that, as these tests proved negative, you are in the clear.

Go back to the clinic for reassurance from professionals, if it would settle your mind. You don't have to take my word for it. But please do take my word that confession would be a fatal blow to your marriage.

I hope that by confessing to me, your conscience will be eased. You've been punishing yourself for years. Now the time has come to forgive yourself, for I'm sure your husband would never be able to.

Threatened by a teen seducer

Dear Marje

Since I lost my wife, I have lived a solitary life. We had a very loving marriage and I cannot describe how much I miss her. I am now 65 and no longer very mobile. A young girl aged 17 does some shopping and errands for me. One afternoon a few weeks ago, she came and sat beside me on the sofa and started kissing and fondling me. I lost all control and made love to her.

She is quite shameless. She undresses as soon as she arrives – and undresses me. I am ashamed of my ageing body, but she says she loves it.

She's been on the Pill, she says, for a year. I have said it must stop because of her youth, but she has threatened to tell her father I seduced her if I forbid her to come here. Now I live in daily fear of discovery.

Says Marje

I can understand why you are so nervous about the possibility of being shopped by your teenage visitor, but I don't see why you should feel so guilty.

This precocious girl set about seducing you with the expertise of an experienced woman twice her age.

I'd advise you to lie back and enjoy it, if it wasn't for that nasty threat. And from the sound of her, she wouldn't hesitate to carry it out.

If she's been on the Pill for a year, presumably you are not her first lover.

I think that if push came to shove, she'd have a hard time convincing her father you'd robbed her of her maidenhood. But I wouldn't want you to take a chance on him coming round and roughing you up.

Your ageing limbs are clearly not a turn-off. It's a mistake to presume that only young and beautiful people make good lovers. You proved that's not true.

Certainly you must try to put a stop to what's happening, though it means some sacrifice. Consider what you'll lose against what you'll gain.

The sexual gratification, for instance. You'll no longer need to feel guilty, but you'll be lonely again and you'll be limping off to do your own shopping.

It's a hard choice to make, and even harder to figure out how to be rid of her. I doubt if she'd carry out her threat, so call her bluff. Refuse to open the door to her and pretend to be out, and let's hope it works.

A lot of men would grab what's on offer and make the most

of it while it lasts. She'll soon be looking for new men, leaving you with wistful memories and much gratitude for the bliss you never dreamed you'd know again.

Betrayal a wife can never forget

Dear Marje

I always trusted my husband, there was no reason not to. We had a great marriage. We celebrated our 10th anniversary with a party and I overheard some banter between my husband and one of the guests.

My suspicions were aroused and I asked him if there was someone else. I expected a denial but he admitted it was true. He says he'd only been with her five times and he'd hated himself for it and he begged me to forgive him. He swore he loved me and promised never to see her again.

He actually gave me a couple of her photos and three letters and we tore them up together. He said that would be a symbolic gesture to prove she meant nothing to him and I honestly believe the affair is over. But I can't forget, though I've forgiven.

I seek reassurance from him all the time, although I know I'm getting on his nerves.

Last night he yelled at me to bloody well stop nagging. He says I'm doing more damage to our marriage than he ever did.

Please help me to cope with this nightmare.

Says Marje

I suppose your husband figured that the symbolic destruction of the other woman's photos and letters would wipe out the affair and you'd carry on as usual presenting a perfect picture of a harmonious couple to the world and yourselves. If only the memory of his infidelity could so easily be wiped from the slate. The torn-up scraps of her pictures and letters, thrown in the bin, can't erase in a few minutes the knowledge that he slept with someone else.

Letter after letter from women like yourself and from men who have been betrayed by a partner they'd trusted, confirm that while forgiving may not be too difficult, forgetting takes a long, long time. Possibly a lifetime. Your husband's accusation that your nagging and need for reassurance is more damaging to your marriage than his affair left me gobsmacked. What he means is that the nagging is a constant reminder of his infidelity and so it is, of course.

He wants to put it all behind him. You are keeping the wound open. And if you continue to nag, he is quite likely to end up blaming you for the affair, implying it's no wonder a man who has to put up with a nagging wife looks around for a bit of the other elsewhere. And it wouldn't do you the least bit of good to point out if it hadn't been for his bit of the other, there'd be no cause for you to nag.

A husband in a similar situation once said to me: "I don't know why she's making such a fuss. I told her I was sorry." I guess your husband takes a similar view.

It's in your own best interest to try to pretend that happy days are here again. Countless marriages like yours do survive but it takes an Oscar-winning performance to sustain them. The success of yours will, I guess, depend on how good an actress you can be.

Wife's toyboy teacher

Dear Marje

I had a good job in a company that collapsed and at 46 I was unemployed and bored.

My daughter is away at college and my husband said I ought to go to adult education classes to occupy my mind.

He also made snide remarks about how it might get rid of my "spare tyres" to use up some energy. My husband, who long ago lost interest in sex, would be surprised how effectively I am now using up energy.

One of the other students is a 25-year-old man and we are doing a lot of "homework" at his lodgings.

I'd forgotten how wonderful lovemaking could be. I call him my "toyboy" and that's what he was to start with. He says I'm cuddly and he's mad about those "spare tyres". But he's getting very serious. He says he loves me as if he means it and he wants to marry me. I'm tempted but I'm scared and I don't know where to go from here. Please, I need some advice.

Says Marje

I am tempted, too, to advise you to say to hell with everything and enjoy what life could offer with your toyboy. But sweet reason has overcome my temptation to say go ahead and ditch your marriage and start again with this young man. Although there are advantages in such a relationship, there are hazards, too. The greatest is the 21-year difference in your age.

Look 20 years ahead, if you can bear to. You will be 66, a pensioner with a bus pass. He will be 45, still a comparatively young man. And although there are some female senior citizens with plenty of sexual vigour, they are in a fairly small minority.

It's impossible to guess whether your toyboy would cherish his loved one in her old age.

When couples grow old together, they may grow old grumpily. They may be sour and quarrelsome, but there's usually an in-built support system that keeps them going.

There are the shared experiences of marriage, of parenthood, of managing in times of stress.

There'd be very few shared experiences between you and your young lover beyond heavy breathing.

Whatever I say I guess you'll continue with your romps. You get such little joy from your husband, I suppose you can forgive yourself for looking for it elsewhere.

But the young man who likes your plump waist and well-rounded hips may unconsciously regard you as a mother-figure. That's a commonplace reason why young men fall for much older women.

You don't want to spend the rest of your life mothering him, do you? Or trying desperately to hide from him the inevitable ravages of time? The most sensible thing you can do is enrol at a different school next term.

Testing time for randy husband

Dear Marje

I am in a terrible state. My moods alternate between rage, bitterness and anxiety. After nearly 20 years of what I believed was a happy marriage I have discovered my husband has had another woman for the past seven years.

I found out because he left the woman's farewell letter in a suit I was taking to the cleaners. From the letter it appears she went with several men as well as my husband which is why he ditched her.

He has admitted it all and promises he'll do anything to preserve our marriage and because I, too, want our marriage to survive I am doing my utmost to put it behind me.

The main problem now is sex. I am terrified although he swears he always used a condom.

Would I be justified in insisting he got tested? I know I can't respond to him in bed unless he does. Do you think I should give him an ultimatum?

Says Marje

I have never been very keen on ultimatums. You put yourself at a disadvantage. If the ultimatum is given a flat turn-down, for where do you go from there?

Sweet reason is likely to get a more positive result. There is a lot of discussion needed in this situation and a few vital questions to be asked.

One is why your husband wanted this other woman when he was apparently so happily married to you?

Often the reason is because a man wants to indulge in practices he believes his wife wouldn't tolerate. Remember it's generally regarded as easier for a man to have sex without emotional commitment than it is for a woman.

You seem convinced that if only your husband was HIV tested and the result was negative, you would then be able to make love to him again. I'm not so sure about that.

I can't prophecy what the result of the test would be but since he used condoms, it should have been safe. What you can't know is whether he's telling the truth about that. He deceived you for seven years.

I wonder, too, about that letter and if it was sheer carelessness or if he hoped to bring his past out in the open, win your forgiveness and thus be able to shed his guilt. We'll never know, will we?

Anyhow, now you do know and since he's promised to do

everything possible to preserve the marriage, your demand for an HIV test should put his promise to the test. If he refuses, there'll be serious problems.

Sex will be the biggest because you'll refuse it, won't you? The survival of your marriage is mainly down to him. But even if his health is pronounced perfect, you face a battle, together, to sort out the reasons for his defection and find the answers if you can.

Incidentally, he can get that test by going to the special clinic at a local hospital.

Now his luck has run out

Dear Marje

A year ago I counted myself lucky. I had a good business which my wife helped to run and our marriage was good, too.

Then the business failed, we got into debt and had to move the children to a state school, which they hate. I started drowning my sorrows and in a moment of drunken madness had a brief affair with a neighbour who, of course, made sure my wife found out.

The stupid thing was it meant nothing. I couldn't even get an erection.

My wife has just announced she's divorcing me. I know I have only myself to blame, except that it wasn't my fault the business went down the pan. I daresay many people blame the recession for their personal failures.

I love my wife and with her help I could have sorted things out. Without her my life won't be worth living. Can you see any hope for me?

Says Marje

Many people blame the recession for everything that goes wrong with their lives and you are right when you apportion some of the blame on forces outside of your control.

But be fair. No one but you was responsible for the fact that you got drunk and bedded your neighbour.

It's true that a depressed economy produces depressed men who, out of anxiety or defeat, can't get it up. But yours seems to have been a case of brewer's droop, plus guilt. It was sheer bloody stupidity to do it with a blabbermouth neighbour. Wives often close a blind eye to a husband's occasional infidelity, as long as they're not forced to acknowledge it.

Do you remember that advice fathers used to pass on to their sons about not doing nasties on their own doorsteps? Clearly your father didn't pass on this wisdom to you.

Incidentally, I hope you'll try to instill some wisdom into your children. Like teaching them that unpleasant little snobs like they appear to be grow up to be very unpopular adults.

Sorry, I've digressed, thinking about their future instead of yours. There's not a lot, actually, that you can do other than plead with your wife to give you a second chance.

The neighbour incident was, I suspect, the last straw. A wife who loves her husband isn't likely to chuck away a marriage because of one foolish, drunken peccadillo.

Perhaps she lost respect when you weren't able to cope with the business failure. But she was your partner and she's a pretty fair-weather partner, great when all was going well but resentful when the going got tough.

You must both accept your share of the blame. I hope your efforts to rebuild your marriage succeed. If not you can always blame the recession.

Knock knock – it's the sexy postie

Dear Marje

There was no excuse for what I did. I wasn't a bored housewife, my husband doesn't drink or knock me about and as far as I know he hasn't slept around, though I've had my suspicions once or twice.

A few months ago, I had a brief fling with our postman, until he was transferred to another depot. He was stupid enough to tell his wife and I'm sure she was behind the move and I really don't blame her. In her shoes I'd have done the same. But she did something else to get her revenge.

She sent my husband an anonymous letter asking him if he knows how often the postal van was parked outside our house and for a lot longer than it takes to deliver a parcel. My husband went berserk.

I denied we'd had an affair and said sometimes I gave the man a cup of coffee or let him use the loo. My husband has vowed to track him down and I'm terrified and desperately need some advice.

Says Marje

And I am desperately beating my brains out trying to think of some useful advice to give you. And not, so far, getting any brilliant inspiration.

I am trying to make excuses for you but there aren't any, are there?

If you'd fallen in love with this postman whose deliveries were apparently so satisfactory, you could at least claim there'd been a valid reason. But since it was merely an occasional bonk, it had no great emotional commitment.

You fancied a bit of the other and you got it. You behaved in fact like large numbers of men, including no doubt your husband, behave. But men who enjoy a little fling now and then take their right to do so for granted. When women do it, society frowns heavily and they are condemned by both women and men. Particularly men, who are very hypocritical about such matters.

Although you tell me you reckon your husband's been at it once or twice, you didn't pack your bags and flounce off. It appears you didn't even protest. Yet here he is, vowing vengeance.

An idea has just occurred to me. Can't you track down the postie, or better still his wife, before your husband finds him? Then write to her. Not aggressively or defensively, just apologetically, begging her forgiveness and her mercy.

Appeal to her better nature and let's hope she has one. Persuade her, if you can, to tell your husband she made up that letter simply out of mischief. I realise this is a long shot. Your best hope is that neither you nor your husband will ever find the postman and that if you continue to deny that his morning visits were anything more than a quick visit to the loo, he'll eventually believe you.

All this will have taught you the lesson many people have to learn:

There's often a very big price to pay for a little passing fun.

Revenge of a lecher's wife

Dear Marje

For most of the 14 years I've been married I've had affairs, I've lost count of how many.

I'm not boasting, it's just that I am polygamous. I can't stay faithful to one woman.

It might be hard to believe, but my wife, who is very easygoing, has never suspected. Then, after one careless slip, she confronted me and like a fool, I confessed. She took it all quite calmly.

Now she just as calmly tells me she has started an affair with a colleague at work. She also says she's thinking of leaving me.

What beats me is her attitude. No ranting or raving, no recriminations. I have sworn I love only her, that the other women were meaningless sex objects and I've promised to

reform. But she just smiles sweetly and says women have rights, too, and the right she claims is to have as many lovers as she fancies.

I honestly want to save my marriage. Can you help?

Says Marje

You're anxious to save your marriage. What marriage? If you mean you are anxious to maintain a relationship which for 14 years has been completely selfish and one-sided, I'm sorry, but you'll get no help from me. A man like you who appears to regard polygamy as some sort of incurable disease over which you have no control, is not good husband material.

I assume you realised before you proposed to your wife that you were a victim of your insatiable lust. Therefore, you married her under false pretences, making a vow on your wedding day you knew you'd be breaking as soon as the honeymoon was over. If not before while, perhaps, she left you for an hour to get her hair done.

I shake my head in wonderment that you are now so outraged because your wife has begun to play your game. So far, it appears she's had only the one lover. But she, too, might fancy a bit of variety as she gets a taste for sex without commitment.

It always amazes me how angry men become when women behave the way men assume they – men – are fully entitled to behave.

You take it for granted that polygamy is OK for you, but your wife must be monogamous, staying faithful to you, though you can have it away with as many women as you can grab hold of. You talk of your polygamy like it's an infectious disease and in a way, that's what it seems to have become. Your wife, it appears, may have caught it.

I expect she is sick and tired of masculine double standards. If your wife does take off, you can blame yourself and your indifference to her happiness.

She might relent and give you the chance to reform, but don't bank on it. Perhaps her regret now is that she'd remained immune from this "illness" for so long, when she too could have enjoyed polygamous away games.

I hope you're both aware of the possibility of that even more fatal illness – Aids.

68

Husband's touches
make her sick

Dear Marje

I got married at 16 and had three children by the time I was 20 and my marriage was perfect in every way. He died just before our fifth anniversary.

For several years I struggled on, bringing up my children, managing somehow on a small wage. The kids were happy, but I was desperately lonely.

A friend introduced me to a very pleasant divorced man. He had a nice large house, was well-off and he was super to my children.

We married four years ago and though I liked him I didn't love him. The children were thrilled. He is the kindest person in the world, but making love with him is like a dreadful nightmare.

I fake orgasm but have never had one with him. I can't bear him entering me, I feel physically sick. It's like being raped and I have to take a shower when he's through.

Sometimes I masturbate but it makes me feel dirty and cheap. I am desperate to know what to do.

Says Marje

It won't do you a lot of good if I remind you that you married this nice man for all the wrong reasons. It's sad, though, that you've now got everything you longed for, except good sex. But I am not as pessimistic about your marriage as you are. I see hope, if you are prepared to work at it.

First, let's get the rape business into proportion.

Your husband penetrates you with your consent. He is entitled to believe he's welcome. While I wouldn't dream of suggesting you tell him intercourse makes you feel physically sick, I think you must talk to him about the sexual problems you face.

I'd guess that sexually you are living in the past, still wanting the young husband and lover you lost, perhaps subconsciously blaming the present one for not being him. Perhaps you even resent your present husband because your children love him so much.

You may wonder what all this has to do with going to bed with him but I think it is relevant. If you can reach orgasm by masturbating, there's nothing wrong with your sexual response.

No one can love another person simply because it's convenient to do so. But you married this man because he'd be a convenient husband, stepfather and provider.

I reckon he's getting a raw deal. Don't think, though, that I blame or condemn you. I just feel it would be tragic if you can't sort this thing out.

If my rambling thoughts have failed to inspire you to try to solve the problem yourself, ask your GP to refer you to a sex therapist.

As for feeling dirty and cheap when you masturbate, that's a commonplace reaction and is the result of unnecessary feelings of guilt and self-hatred.

Forget all that. If it satisfies your sexual needs, for the moment carry on doing it and enjoying it.

Hell for this sinning wife

Dear Marje

My husband and I met when I was 12 and he was 14. We got married when I was 20 and though there was no passion, there was love.

We had two children in the first five years and I was happy except that I longed for that missing passion. My husband had a low sex drive and would rather use his energy for sport. He is a once-a-month man, if I'm lucky.

About 12 years after I married, I met another man and we had an affair which lasted only a few months, for I was deeply guilty and I ended it. In a fit of remorse, I confessed to my husband.

He went crazy and said he'd divorce me but he relented and "forgave" me, and my life has been hell ever since.

He continually reminds me of my "sin". Since my confession, sex has been like a punishment. But oddly, he wants it more and more often. Now, at 37, I am trying to decide whether I should leave him. What do you think?

Dear Marje

I noticed you put the word "forgave" in quotes. This implies you realised that your husband's forgiveness was really the beginning of your punishment.

If you continue to live with your husband, your punishment, I fear, will be a life sentence. That's what you fear too and I don't think you'd get far if you begged for mercy.

You are quite right when you say he's now using sex as his main instrument of punishment.

It's his only effective method of making you suffer for the indignity you heaped on him, and his anger stimulates his desire. How I wish you'd been able to resist the temptation to confess, thus saving him the loss of face.

I feel immensely sorry for him while understanding why you had that affair. After all, you did try hard to get him to see how sexually frustrated you were and if he hadn't been both blind and foolish, he'd have been less into whatever sport he enjoyed and more into satisfying your needs.

One of the problems of youthful romances that end in happy-ever-after marriages, is that because of the inexperience of the couple, the marriages often end all too unhappily. As has happened in your case.

But before you make the decision I believe you'll reach, which is to leave him and try to start life again in your forties, consider your children. A parting now would disrupt their young lives, with possible disastrous effects.

You've taken your punishment for a long time and although it's been very tough going, maybe on reflection you'll think its worth while continuing to take it until you feel your children are old enough to cope with the parting.

Leaving him will probably be the best thing for your husband. He, too, will have a second chance of happiness.

And let's hope he'll find someone who shares his interest in sport and doesn't bother unduly about the indoor variety.

Secret baby still haunts her

Dear Marje

A year ago I fell in love and we decided to live together

71

before getting married. We have now fixed a date for our wedding and if it wasn't for an awful cloud hanging over my life, I would be ecstatic.

When I was still at college, I had a baby by a married family friend, a man I trusted almost as a father. I can't really say he seduced me – I was too young and ignorant to realise what was happening.

My baby was born just before my 18th birthday (I am now 24) and was adopted. I was really given no choice, although parting with her was terrible.

Now that I am about to marry the man I love, I am in a terrible dilemma. Should I tell him? Will this secret spoil my life if I don't? I desperately need advising, please.

Says Marje

It's plain that your secret is already spoiling your life. You've had six years of a secret hell and now you have a wonderful opportunity to bring that secret out into the open.

By telling your husband-to-be what happened, you'd be taking a chance that he'd be understanding and supportive, but I think the risk to your marriage would be even greater if he remained in ignorance.

The guilt and sadness at the loss of your baby will always remain with you but I hope there's some comfort in knowing she is being brought up by two people who will love her.

Reading between the lines of your letter, there seems to have been a strong element of shame, encouraged by your parents and your baby's very nasty father.

I think it's that which is so damaging to you. And I feel that once you've been able to unload that secret, the black cloud will slowly disperse.

You ask me if I think the man you love has to know. There's no compulsion to tell him but I believe you should. A marriage based on deceit 'and secrets is bound to be an imperfect one.

There would always be an underlying fear that somehow he might find out. Who knows, in 20 years or so a young girl could appear on your doorstep saying she's your long-lost daughter.

Many adopted children seek out their mothers and I've heard heart-rending stories of natural parents who reject those long-lost offspring because their births had remained secret. You will be far less likely to be haunted by the knowledge that someone else is rearing your child if your secret is shared with the man you love and trust.

Guilty secret of twenty years

Dear Marje

When I was seven my parents took me to stay with an uncle and aunt for our summer holiday. I will never ever forget it. Their children – my cousins – were older than me and I felt lonely for most of the time. But I worshiped my 16-year-old cousin and trailed around after him all the time. Then one day he took me up to his bedroom and pulled my knickers down and exposed himself. I was very scared. I had no idea what he was doing. Actually he didn't do anything, he pushed me out of the room.

I didn't tell anyone, in fact I've kept it to myself for 20 years. But now he's getting married and I'm worried. Will his children be at risk if I don't speak up, and anyway who would I tell?

Is a man who exposes himself to a child a threat to other children, including his own, for the rest of his life?

Says Marje

I do not know what compels some men to expose themselves. There are probably many different reasons and many theories. I am no expert in this matter.

But I do know what a frightening experience it is for the victims of men who suddenly unzip and flash their genitals – frightening and deeply unnerving.

Especially for a child of seven, as you were when your cousin demonstrated, perhaps for the first time in your young life, the physical difference between males and females.

Thank goodness he went no further than unzipping, at any rate while you were in the room. I suspect, though obviously I'm only guessing, that as soon as he shut the door he masturbated.

I think his exposure was probably a spur of the moment need for relief. But I can understand why you are worried now and why this anxiety has festered. You don't say whether or not you have a man in your life or whether you've had any relationships but an incident like this could mar a partnership.

Although you've kept it secret for 20 years, it's not too late to talk about it now – not to take retribution on your cousin, but to help you.

I advise you to ring Childline on 0800 1111 (a 24-hour Freephone counselling service). It doesn't matter that you are adult. They will refer you on for appropriate counselling.

As for your cousin, my guess is that he has grown out of his need to expose himself and I don't think you should continue to fret over him.

I'm optimistic enough to believe that a randy 16-year-old can develop into a decent, responsible 36-year-old husband and father who has long since forgotten that adolescent incident.

I hope to goodness that I'm right.

Boozy romp with his wife's friend

Dear Marje

I've got myself into a right mess. My wife walked out several weeks ago because of my constant two-timing and the night she left I was so upset I ended up bingeing in the pub. I got completely drunk and as I was staggering home, a car stopped. It was one of my wife's friends and she offered me a lift. When we got to my place she made me a coffee and an offer. God knows why, but I accepted.

This woman is an attractive divorcee, but honestly, I don't fancy her. But when she took off her clothes and mine, we had sex right there on the floor.

I am terrified she'll tell my wife, who's just come back to me and wants us to try again. But I know I'll lose her for good if she finds out. Would it be wise of me to confess in case this woman blabs?

Says Marje

I am not much in favour of confession as a rule. Sometimes it helps to clear the air. Other times it can pollute it. While

74

confession helps to ease the conscience of the sinner, it can cause unnecessary pain and suffering to an innocent party. I can't possibly imagine how your wife would react.

As we are all aware, having regard for certain recent newsworthy events, some saintly wives forgive the most blatant of matrimonial offences.

"Stand by your man" seems to have become a universal theme song, and although it's very noble and all that, it's dangerous to assume every wife is similarly saintly. Perhaps yours is.

But if you are in any doubt, I'd say keep mum.

You were a fool but you were drunk and, while that's no excuse, it's a reason.

And since the reason why your wife left you was because you'd been sleeping around, it won't endear you to her to be told you were at it as soon as her back was turned.

Confess, and she'll probably pack her bags again. You must pray her friend will keep her mouth shut. Hopefully, she'll feel some shame and regret.

What amazes me is how you managed to perform in your condition.

Obviously no brewer's droop there.

When a man gets himself as near as paralytic as you were, he's only usually fit for several hours of oblivion. You'll have to live with the uncertainty of exposure.

It's part of the penance to be paid, not only for one drunken sin, but for all the previous ones.

It would be sensible to ask yourself why you needed those other women – if it was merely for kicks, or to notch up successes, or because you weren't getting what you needed from your wife.

It might be sensible for her to consider those questions, too.

Sexy thoughts make her feel dirty

Dear Marje

After my divorce five years ago I picked myself up and made a huge effort to rebuild my life. I have succeeded – I

75

think! During my marriage I had an active and enjoyable sex life but when it ended, that was that.

I didn't miss sex and I rarely thought about it. My job takes up all my time and energy.

But about a month or so ago, I began to get sexually excited again.

There seemed to be no particular reason for these disturbing feelings.

Now I find that when I'm watching some steamy film or TV show I can hardly control myself.

I have started looking reflectively at the men at work and even men I see in the street or when I go shopping.

It's not a bit like me. It makes me feel sort of dirty and I don't know what to to do about it.

I'm scared that it would only be a matter of time before I actually pick someone up – a thought that absolutely horrifies me.

Says Marje

I think I can guess why you have suddenly rediscovered the joy of sex. Or rather the joy you'd get out of it if you could get it.

You don't mention your age but I'd say this sudden surge and urge is probably due to the pre-menopausal activity of hormones which are telling you there's still a hell of a lot of mileage in you yet. And why knock it?

I can understand that you feel vulnerable – on account of the fact that you are.

But dirty? Come off it. It would only become dirty if you picked up a dubious man.

It is definitely not a good idea to wander around the supermarket assessing the possibilities of male shoppers.

As for the men at work you do at any rate, have a chance to size them up, so to speak. But before you make any move, check out if they're married or spoken for or gay.

I see no reason why a woman like you shouldn't look for a nice man as long as you don't break up an established relationship.

That could all end in tears for you as well as for the man.

Your biggest problem will be to find a suitable partner and if you don't manage that soon you'll be in danger of picking an unsuitable one. Many people have found soul and bed mates through introduction agencies. The good ones don't come cheap.

It's sensible to use only those affiliated to the Association of British Introduction Agencies, 25 Abingdon Road, London W8 6AH.

Some people express doubt about meeting partners this way. It seems like an admission of inadequacy. I don't go along with that.

If you meet a stranger by this method, he'd be likewise using the same method to meet you.

All this will take time to organise. Meanwhile you can satisfy your urges for the moment with a little self-help.

Because your body will sensitively respond to your own efforts, masturbation is often even better than the real thing.

Isn't he entitled to bliss?

Dear Marje

I have been married for 26 years to a wife I have loved since I was 20. Then five years ago, by chance I met another woman at a trade conference.

She was a very lovely but very unhappy woman. She was going through a traumatic divorce at the time and it was obvious she needed someone to talk to and I just happened to be around.

Neither of us planned it, but our friendship turned into love and we are still desperately in love. When we are together the atmosphere is electric. We read each other's thoughts and share each other's interest. Sex is bliss.

She has never asked me to leave my wife and children because she knows the pain of divorce. But wouldn't you agree that I am now entitled to happiness with the woman I will love forever?

Says Marje

Two points I must raise with you. First, the claim that you are entitled to happiness. I'm always puzzled when people make this claim. I don't understand the entitlement.

Happiness, surely, is a bonus we enjoy at unforgettable moments in time. The rest of life goes at a sort of jogalong pace and you're lucky if it's reasonably contented.

I get very alarmed when people plan to shed all they've got for this fleeting, ephemeral happiness.

My second point is to do with love. You say you've loved your wife for 26 years. Presumably, she too was the woman you vowed to love forever.

But forever lasted only a quarter of a century, and now here you are, girding yourself for yet another forever with your mistress.

She sounds like a very nice woman. Too nice to put any pressure on you to leave your wife and children. I think that when you go – as I'm sure you will, whatever I say – she'll be nice enough to feel guilty about your wife. As you say, she knows all about the agony of rejection and divorce.

Think about that before you pack your bags. Her remorse could be something of a blight on that happiness. And it would undoubtedly take the edge off the bliss for you, too.

You might have to face anger and disgust from your children, although with divorce and family disruption now so commonplace, maybe they'll just shrug with boredom.

After all, they'll be no different from so many of their school friends.

So who knows what may happen as a result of that meeting five years ago? I hope you'll never regret that it occurred.

But since it did, since it changed your life and the lives of at least four other people, all you can do now is go on paying forever – one way or another – for the consequences.

Mistress cheats on her lover

Dear Marje

When I met my mistress seven years ago, I told her I would never leave my wife and children for I have a strong sense of duty.

My mistress accepted these conditions. We have – or had – a highly satisfactory relationship. I bought her a flat, paid her an allowance and she has a part-time job to give her something to do when I cannot be with her. I am a 55-year-old businessman and she is 32.

She has now told me there is another man. He is six years her junior and she refused to give him up despite my anger. Her argument is that if I can lead a double life, so can she. She will not discuss if they have sex.

I have threatened to sell the flat and stop her allowance but she knows me well enough to realise these are empty threats. I doubt if you can help me but I believe it might be worth a try. Thank you.

Says Marje

Dear Sir, Thank you in turn for your business-like letter. Except for one tiny hint of an emotional involvement with your mistress, you write almost as if you are recording the minutes of a board meeting.

The word love appears not to be part of your crisp vocabulary, although clearly sex is.

You do not say whether or not you still practice it with your wife, though precise and correct as you are, I imagine you provide a service for the woman who keeps your home fires burning and makes sure the kids wash behind the ears.

Frankly, I do not see how you can refute your mistress's argument. What she says is perfectly reasonable and she's simply playing the old goose and gander game.

For years she has been a sex-object and although I daresay she appreciated the home you paid for and the pocket money you gave her, I imagine she'd reckon she paid a high price to be little more than a superannuated call-girl, providing you have exclusive right to her body between your business meetings.

Perhaps her new boyfriend makes her feel valued as a real person, not merely a kept person. Maybe what she'd missed these past seven years was a sense of real worth as distinct from material worth.

If she is expected to share you with your wife, logically you should be prepared to share her with her boyfriend.

It looks like you'll have to accept that he's now part of her life, as your family is part of yours.

But if you can't, I hope you won't remove the roof over her head. You could surely put that down to regrettable loss of working capital.

Bled dry by a bimbo

Dear Marje

I have paid and paid for a sin I committed nearly 30 years ago.

I'd just got married when I met a young girl and we had sex. She persuaded me to take nude pictures of her and she took several of me.

Later I discovered that she was only 15. She has blackmailed me ever since. After she got married, her demands for money continued. Her husband left her and she asked for even more. I have tried to persuade my wife to move away from our home but she loves it and can't understand why I want to leave.

Apart from that one time, I have never been unfaithful to the wife I love. But I don't believe I could ever tell her that I betrayed her. It was a criminal as well as an utterly stupid act which I will always regret.

I am now 55 and money is tight, but this woman is relentless and I know that if I stop paying she will post those pictures to my wife.

Says Marje

You don't actually have many options. You must either continue to submit to this outrageous blackmailer or call her bluff, tell her the account is now closed and take the risk that she'll carry out her threat. Or tell your wife.

That would be my recommendation. You say you don't believe you could tell your wife, but it's difficult to believe that a wife you've loved for 30 years would sling you out because you strayed briefly so long ago.

I so detest blackmailers that in your shoes I'd see that bloody woman in hell before I paid her another penny.

And if you continue to give in so weakly to her demands you will never get off the hook on which she has so cleverly trapped you.

You'll be sending her your retirement pension in a few years. I think you can now safely forget about her under-age status. You weren't aware of it at the time and you aren't likely to be caged up now because of it. If you do manage to brace yourself to tell your wife, you can conveniently forget the age business.

It does occur to me that in 30 years your appearance will have changed a lot.

Any chance, do you think, of insisting it must have been some other unclothed lad if your blackmailer posts those snaps? Just an idle thought.

I want very much to get you off that cruel hook and I hope you'll tell your wife all – or nearly all – and beg her forgiveness.

And how wonderful it would be if your wife asked for the address of that nasty piece of work so she could pop round and collect those pictures herself. Another idle thought, I guess. But you never know – or you won't unless you find the strength to tell your tormentor to go to hell and do her worst.

Flirt freezes him out

Dear Marje

I think my wife must be going through the menopause and, believe me, it's a nightmare.

She has taken it into her head that she hates me and, though she flirts with other men and gives them a strong come-on, she won't let me near her, let alone touch her.

As for sex, she says I can forget it. I do everything I can to calm her, but the looks I get freeze the blood. I hardly recognise the woman I love.

I want to be happy again with her. But what's the hope, do you think that once this change of life is over, she'll return to normal? She is 42 and I am 47 and we've just passed our 20th anniversary.

Says Marje

I note you didn't describe your anniversary as a celebration. Sounds like it was a pretty bleak occasion, with you gazing at her in desperation and her glaring with unexplained rage and dislike.

You reckon her menopause is at the back of the problems in your marriage.

But she's only 42 and although some women do start the hot flushes and so forth that young, I think you are simply grabbing at an excuse, rather than a logical reason for the way her feelings have changed towards you.

It's a nice, easy get out for men whose marriages are on the blink to blame the wife's menopause.

And while it's true to say that many women in their late 40s and early 50s suffer unpleasant symptoms, it's also true that some men blame the wife's moods and forget their own shortcomings.

Are you a perfect, nice-to-be-near, sober, romantic, considerate and blameless husband?

Or has she simply gone off you because you've developed a beer belly, snore all night, grab her for a bit of the other when

82

you're in the mood, and never mind whether she is nor not?

You may be as perfect as your letter implies, but it might pay you to take a long, hard look at yourself. Up to now you've only been looking at her.

I can't explain why I'm wondering if there's an element present of what I call the Unfinished Business Syndrome, which is sex that is great for a man and leaves the woman stranded and frustrated. Why, otherwise, would your wife be so openly flirtatious with other men?

Another explanation could be that you've been showing interest elsewhere and she wants to make you jealous. There are endless possibilities, but the plain fact is that she's gone off you. If it's not the menopause, what is it? Try asking her, instead of blaming her. And, on finding the right answers, you might be able to look forward to celebrating your 25th.

No cuddles from a cold wife

Dear Marje

Even before we got married, I realised my wife was not a physical person. She was a virgin on our wedding day and I loved her and still do, although to all intents and purposes she's still a virgin.

Not actually, for we have three children, but she is almost as unapproachable as she was when we met.

We have been married 19 years and she is generous, good-tempered and a wonderful mother. But although she doesn't resist love-making I feel she puts up with it because she's so nice and kind.

We sleep in a double-bed but there's no cuddling or caressing. She has never touched my genitals. I ache for some show of affection from her.

I do not want anyone else. I am not sex-starved, only love-starved. The years ahead in a marriage like ours seem hopeless. I wonder if you have any comments that would help me?

Says Marje

The first comment that comes to mind is: Why doesn't this husband realise how bloody lucky he is? Nothing is ever perfect and those who expect perfection are certain to be disappointed. But for an affectionate man to be married to a woman incapable of expressing her feelings, life must be immensely frustrating.

You imply she lacks feeling. Inhibited she most certainly is, and she is clearly very shy.

It would be interesting to know whether she ever scooped the children up in her arms when they were still of a scoopable age.

When they fell over did she cuddle them and kiss their wounds better? If she was a cold and unaffectionate mother, it would be hard to convince me she was a wonderful one. There's no way of knowing why she's withheld affection from you and I don't think you should take it personally.

If she could tell a psychotherapist the secrets of her own childhood, I daresay clues would emerge. But I can't imagine you'd want to try to persuade her to open that can of worms.

You love her too much to submit her to such painful self-examination which might not, in any case, resolve the problem.

I'm sure it must be boring when someone advises you to count your blessings, but don't yawn. You have no alternative. I can't imagine you'd cast around for another woman to console you and fiddle around with your genitals. I'm now going to make a suggestion which may make you splutter with rage. Why don't you get a dog? Dogs are unquestionably affectionate and the love of a faithful pooch could be a great comfort as you settle into middle-age.

I guarantee that as long as you choose a sloppy one – a spaniel for example – you'd soon be counting him among your blessings, along with your near-perfect wife.

Cruel wife who laughs at his manhood

Dear Marje

I was a happy man until my wife decided she was bored with her dull, staid life.

She started going to hen-parties with the girls at work and it seemed like harmless fun until they went to see some

male strippers. Since then she's never stopped making fun of me.

She keeps going on about how small my penis is. She insists she's joking, and I could take it but for the fact that she makes jokes about how well-endowed these other blokes are compared to me. I'm finding it very hard to laugh it off.

Last night she brought home a porn mag, full of pictures of men with huge penises. We've always had a great sex life but now I'm so lacking in confidence that I often fail to get an erection. She accuses me of having lost my sense of humour and it's becoming obvious that not only our sex life is threatened, but our marriage is too, and I am desperate to know what to do about it.

Says Marje

I can't help wondering if your sex life and your marriage were really quite as wonderful as you'd assumed they were.

Your wife was bored. Her life was dreary and she looked around for something to relieve the boredom and found fun by going to hen-parties. And by gazing enviously at the well-hung males on display.

Countless women get harmless kicks this way. They fantasise about how it would be touch rather than merely to look at these well-oiled bodies who prance around so provocatively for their amusement.

The irony of it all is that, if these sex-hungry women did but know it, many of the beefy boys are gay. To them, the sexy gyrations they perform at hen-parties are simply a job for which they get paid.

As far as they're concerned, they could be bus drivers or bank clerks. Their bodies just happen to be commercially valuable.

But tell that to the women who scream with delight when they ripple their muscles, and you'd be wasting your breath.

I think your wife is a cruel, unimaginative woman who is now deliberately making you suffer for the years of boredom you mistook for years of bliss.

When she jokes about the size of your penis she is deliberately trying to denigrate you in every way.

If what she is doing to you is her idea of humour, she is

pretty nasty and doesn't deserve the love you have for her. I think you're in a no-win situation here.

Your penis probably is small compared to some of these freaks she lusts after. But I bet it sizes up perfectly well to the national average.

All I can suggest is you do try to laugh off her sneers and ignore them if you can. Certainly don't rise to them (no pun intended).

And I hope she'll read this and take warning that if she's not careful, she could end up alone – with only porn-mag pin-ups for very cold company.

Led a merry dance by his mistress

Dear Marje

It all began at a company dinner dance, where my wife and I met a colleague's daughter. She was 21 and I was 47. We danced and I can't describe what it was like that first time I held her. I left my wife to live with her and it was marvellous. I'd forgotten that sex could be so intense.

But, and it's a story I'm sure you've heard before, she's having an affair with another man. We've lived together for three years and now she intends to leave me for him. Surprisingly he's no young stud; he's about my age.

I am devastated. My wife (we're still married) had a nervous breakdown. I gave up my home and my children for a girl who doesn't know the meaning of the word loyalty.

How can I make her see she's putting her future at risk if she leaves me for him?

Says Marje

You are right. I have heard various versions of your story before and although this kind of relationship does sometimes work, more often than not it ends in tears.

Usually running down the cheeks of the man.

What's a bit unusual in your case is that the girl is leaving you for another 50-year-old. As a rule, when a middle-aged man suffers a sexual decline, a girl looks for kicks from a younger, more virile partner.

But your girl is not, I think, going for sex. She wants a father. Don't ask me why. I'd have to know more about her childhood and her parents to make a guess.

Any girl can tell you how easy it is to pull an older man if she puts her mind and her thighs and breasts to it.

As yours did at that dinner dance. Men of your age, with jog-along marriages, are a gift.

And incidentally if I may say so – and I will, whether or not I may – who are you to whinge about loyalty? Where was yours when you abandoned your wife? I wouldn't advise you to use that accusation in an attempt to stop your girl leaving you. I doubt, though, if you'll succeed, whatever arguments you use. She'll probably hang around with the next one for a few more years until she starts looking yet again, forever searching for the father she wants so much more than she wants a lover.

I noted you mentioned you and your wife are still married. Did that, I wonder, denote a tiny hope that you might be able to kiss and make up with her after your girl departs? Don't bank on it. You may still be legally married, but your wife must now have got used to life without the man who rejected her.

And who knows, she may in her lonely days and nights be enjoying the comfort of a nice, friendly man in his 20s. I admit I do rather hope so.

Secret desire of a postie

Dear Marje

You had a letter on your page recently about a young wife who fancied the postman. The reason I am writing to you is that I'm a postman who fancies a young wife.

When I deliver the mail to their address, I'm praying there'll be a large package so I can ring the doorbell and, if I'm lucky, she'll open up. Sometimes her husband comes to the door and spoils my day.

Believe it or not, I am 53 and a happily married man and I suppose you'll give me an ear-wigging and tell me to act my age. But this girl does something to me. The daft thing

87

is I've never even said more than: "morning, rain again", or similar. She might be a right little vixen if I got any further. To tell you the truth, I don't even know if I'd want it if I was offered it on a plate.

I don't even know why I'm writing this, except I feel I must tell someone. Thanks a lot.

Says Marje

It's nice of you to thank me, though I don't know why you should, except I think you are a funny, nice man.

If only there were more like you to give me a giggle on a muggy Monday morning.

I wish you were my postie. I'd certainly be there to open the door to have a natter about the weather.

I am definitely not about to give you an ear-wigging. Why would I?

Although you are somewhat rocked on your heels by this lady of the house, I'm relieved to know you are not sufficiently rocked to be actually lusting after her.

It's very civilised to want to exchange a few amiable words with her so that you can continue on your lonely round with a song in your heart.

It's a harmless pastime for an appreciative man who enjoys the finer things of life, like pleasant ladies.

There's no reason why you shouldn't admit to it in your affable, good-natured way, instead of either building up a dangerous fantasy or threatening a woman's peace of mind.

It's sad that we've all got to such a pitch of apprehension in our so-called enlightened society that a decent, happily married man like you can't murmur a polite compliment to an unknown woman without being seen as a threat to her safety or labelled a sexist ratbag. It's just as well, though, to keep a safe distance from that front door.

Her husband could be a heavyweight champ and bad-tempered with it. The family Rottweiler might be growling just inside the door.

A postman can't be too careful.

I am very happy that, even in the unlikely event of an offering on a plate, you'd turn down the offer, though perhaps with some reluctance.

It's an offer most men would grab, without a thought about

the almost inevitable consequences. And thanks a lot to you, too. Have a nice day.

What's happened to his lovely wife?

Dear Marje

I look at my once-lovely, sexy wife and I can't believe that a woman could change so much in only 12 years.

When we got married, she was 20, a slender blonde, a sharp dresser who loved a good time.

She gave up her job to be a wife and mother and we jogged along happily enough. But recently I have found myself looking at my wife like a stranger. Who, I wonder, is this plump, frowsy woman with mouse-coloured hair and a double chin?

She slops around in baggy old T-shirts. And she's never considered going back to work.

The really awful thing is that I no longer want to sleep with her. It's just as well she doesn't seem interested either because I doubt if I could get an erection.

I'm not the sort of man to desert my family because I've gone off my wife, but the prospect ahead is grim.

Says Marje

It is truly sad that a woman can change so much but it doesn't surprise me. It's happening to wives all over the place and as often as not, it's husbands who must share the blame.

Have you ever considered how boring life is for women trapped in the home, doing the endless repetitive chores?

Did it ever occur to you during the past 12 years that housework and trips to the supermarket are not exactly fulfilling? Of course not.

That, you figure – if you figure anything – is what women get married for, and they should be thankful to have a decent home and a faithful provider.

But if your sexy, lovely wife had insisted, 12 years ago, that she'd be the breadwinner while you gave up work to run the home, how would you look today? Fat, no doubt, with a double chin, slopping around in jeans and a baggy old T-shirt, hair all anyhow from pushing it off your sweaty brow. And much too tired to be bothered with sex.

Your wife has deteriorated because she's had no incentive to stay lovely and sexy. I don't suppose you've ever paid her a compliment, even if she didn't merit one.

But an occasional "you look stunning, babe" can do wonders for a woman's morale. Taking her out to dinner once a week would give her a reason to dress up and get her hair done.

My message to her is to have some blonde highlights put in and to try to smarten up and to lose some weight.

I think that if you began to show an interest in her looks again she would, too.

The prospect ahead need not be as grim as you fear. Encourage her to think about going back to part-time work.

That'll be a great incentive for her to go back to full-time living.

And that may well mean full-time loving, too, for both of you. Incidentally, have you changed in the past 12 years?

Are you still the handsome stud that sexy blonde married? I wonder ...

She has lost touch with her feelings

Dear Marje

My girlfriend got in a terrible state when she found out she was pregnant.

She didn't want the baby, she wanted to carry on at college. She was terrified of what her parents would say, she didn't like the idea of adoption and she kept on at me about what to do.

I finally persuaded her to have an abortion. That was about a year ago.

At first she was very depressed but now she's more like her old self except that she won't have sex or let me kiss her or touch her.

She says she loves me and doesn't blame me for the abortion although she's not keen to talk about it.

I'm wild about this girl and I'm hoping we'll get married,

90

but she doesn't want to talk about that either, although she's said she'll marry me when we get a home organised. I'm sure you understand why I need some advice.

Dear Marje

You both need advice – she perhaps more than you. She is allowing you to take over her life, to make decisions that she should be making for herself.

That abortion, for instance. She had it because you urged her to. I'm sure your intentions were good, but it could have been the wrong decision for her. Abortion is a very traumatic experience.

Many women continue to suffer secretly for years and years. They experience terrible guilt. Their relief at disposing – literally – of the problem of an unwanted pregnancy is mixed up with bitter regret about their loss.

Even women who'd do anything to rid themselves of the result of careless sex suffer from this terrible sense of loss.

And mixed up with all these complex emotions are the feelings about the man who was responsible for the pregnancy. For you, the result is twofold. You made your girl pregnant and you persuaded her to abort.

I think that's why she instinctively rejects you physically, even though she loves you. She's torn, it seems to me, between her need for your love and her unconscious revenge for the loss of her child.

If her mother had been the one to advise abortion, she'd have seen you as being on her side, and not against her.

She is, you say, her old self, but she isn't. Her old self would have responded to sex as she did before that pregnancy.

I hope she can come to accept that it takes two to make a baby. In this case, both partners were willing and she must stop blaming you for her depression, her loss and her guilt.

Give her the chance to prove she loves you but try not to pressure her. You can't be expected to wait forever and neither should you. The best thing for your girl would be counselling or psychotherapy which her GP could arrange. This is something else you could persuade her to have.

Meanwhile don't enter into a one-sided marriage which would make your problems – and hers – a million times worse.

Naked lack of loving

Dear Marje

Please believe this is not a hoax letter. I am 21 and split from my boy friend six months ago.

When he left me, I got very depressed and then I met a married man with two children who said he'd like to have a relationship with me, but didn't intend to be unfaithful to his wife. Because I was so lonely, I agreed.

Naturally, I assumed there'd be some sort of sexual element but what happens is, he comes round to my flat for an hour or two, we have a couple of drinks, he takes all his clothes off and likes me to wear only my knickers.

There's not a trace of passion, we just sit there with a glass of wine and talk. I am getting really frustrated. I've tried to touch him but he brushes me aside. He says he wouldn't do anything to hurt his wife.

But he is hurting me, though if I pack him in I'll be alone again. I guess you'll tell me I'll never get anywhere with this man.

Says Marje

Your guess is right. Not only are you very unlikely to get beyond this weird private viewing, you are going to be very hurt when the man becomes bored with the small talk and looks around for someone with a different taste in knickers.

That moment will come when your frustration gets out of control and you make a determined grab for the goods on display.

There is no accounting for strange fetishes. Or rather, I cannot account for this one. I've never encountered it before in a long career of observing rituals many people use to satisfy their sexual fantasies.

Your friend, I imagine, loves himself and his body. He wants to expose it in all its naked glory to the gaze of some admiring young woman who will appreciate its impressive contours. You don't mention if he is anything much to look at. I do not get the impression, somehow, of Chippendale-style rippling muscles.

Neither do you enlighten me about whether he gets an erection as he sips his wine and talks about the weather or the state of the economy.

I suppose he insists on you keeping your knickers on just in case catching an intimate glimpse of you might tempt him to be unfaithful to his wife. It's your knickers, I think which are the this key to this man's strange need. The last thing he wants from you is sex. He simply wants you to look at him. He is the ultimate exhibitionist and you are wasting your time with this far from funny joker.

You are on a hiding to nothing. My advice to you is, next time he turns up at the flat, tell him to stay zipped-up and bid him farewell.

It will be great for your morale and self-esteem if you say goodbye before he does – and it will help you to keep the depression at bay.

That was caused, I think, more by your boyfriend's rejection than by his loss. Now you can even the score by turfing out this weirdo – and you'd be sensible to do it now.

She's starved of love

Dear Marje

I am terribly scared, I think I'm crazy. I am forty. I have constant dreams and fantasies about a man, who in these dreams, is my late father.

In my dreams he hits me and screams at me. There's a lot of yelling and shouting and crying and smacks until I apologise and then he hugs and kisses me. There is no sex in these fantasies.

In his lifetime, my father never showed me any affection, he never hugged or kissed me but he didn't punish me either. Even after all these years, I long for a man's arms to hold me, I crave to be shown love. But I can never picture myself making love with any man I'm attracted to.

I drink alone in the evenings, dangerous, I know, but I

93

feel so hopeless. I am hoping you can see some way that I could break these unnatural dreams. Sometimes I fear they indicate I might even be a "spanking" pervert.

Says Marje

I certainly do not believe you're crazy. You are somewhat disturbed, yes, but the explanation for that seems so simple and logical that you should be able to rationalise it easily.

Your whole life has been clouded by your father's lack of love – or his inability to show love.

From childhood you braced yourself for punishment, for his anger, for a beating. The fact that none of those things happened didn't prevent you from expecting them.

And mingled with your fears was the longing for the consoling hugs you didn't get either.

I think the reason why you close your mind to sexual fulfilment with the father-figures you dream about is because father and daughter sexual intercourse is taboo. I think it's this element of incest that scares you most. Face up to this and you will begin to understand the way your sleeping mind works.

But accepting this proposition doesn't mean you'll go out tomorrow, meet a man and think, "Gee, I fancy him, he's not a bit like my dad" – and make him an offer he'll be happy to accept. But in time I think you will. I wish I could persuade you to lay off the booze, for you won't find the answers through a haze of alcohol.

You begged me for a line telling you if I thought you were crazy. It's taken a good many lines to assure you that I do not.

I'm sure you're not a "spanking" pervert either. You are simply a lonely woman looking for the love you've been avoiding for far too long.

There are plenty of nice men who have nothing whatsoever in common with your late father. It's time now to let him rest in peace. Then you'll find peace yourself.

Bedtime romps ruined marriage

Dear Marje

Divorced, childless and lonely, I couldn't believe my luck when I met a young widow with two small children. A

94

couple of months later, we got married and I was the happiest man in the world and probably the stupidest.

For years I'd had the sort of three-in-a-bed fantasies a lot of men have. We joke about it in the pub.

Although some boast about the great times they have with two women, I never went beyond thinking about it.

My second wife was a fantastic lover, unlike the first, who was more interested in gardening.

One night I told her about my fantasies and she said she'd do it. We had steamy sessions over about six months.

Then one day I got home to find a letter saying she'd had it, she felt disgusted and used. She is now at her mother's and once again I'm alone.

I love her and the children desperately. How can I persuade her to give me a second chance?

Says Marje

I suppose one of the worst things a man can do to the woman who loves him is degrade her. While there are plenty of women willing to participate in erotic sexual practices for the fun of it, when your wife agreed to fulfil your three-in-a-bed fantasy it wasn't, I guess, because she was into weird sex.

It was because she loved you and wanted to make you happy.

What she failed to realise, and you were too thick to understand, was that when another woman came into your bed, love was no longer going to be the name of the game.

It's easy to see why she felt degraded. She felt used because she was used.

You made good use of both women. What a pity you didn't stick to jokes in the pub.

I wonder what the other woman got out of it? And if she, too, felt degraded? Unless of course, she was a hired help, paid to do the job.

Clearly she, unlike your wife, didn't do it for love, which brings us back to where we began: how to persuade her to come back to you. I assume you've already apologised and grovelled but it will, I think, take much more. You must try to convince her that you honestly regret your immature behaviour.

If, in fact, you do regret it. But if you still have this yearning for threesome sex, you'll have to give up trying to save your marriage. If you want your wife and stepchildren even more than you want the fulfilment of your dreams, go to see her, or write to her.

She just might give the marriage another try. I hope she does, for her children's sake as well as hers. And yours. I'd like your sad story to have a happy ending.

And I do hope you've sent a polite thank-you note to that third party explaining why her services are no longer needed.

Victim of a weird pervert

Dear Marje

It's taken me a long time to pluck up courage to write to you. Five years ago, I married a lovely man, or so I thought. He is quiet and kind, is really helpful round the house and with the baby and he never stops telling me how much he loves me.

But within the last year or so he has begun to develop some weird sexual tastes and habits which worry me terribly. I can't even bring myself to describe some of the things he expects me to do. One I will tell you about is that he wants to enter me on all fours like I'm a dog! He also wants to dominate and punish me, though he hasn't yet actually hurt me. I'm always scared and I find it all terribly humiliating.

Yet I'm afraid to leave him with a young baby dependent on me. And in any case, wouldn't it be unfair to deprive her of her father?

Says Marje

A sado-masochist with leanings towards bestiality is probably a fair description of your husband. And it's interesting that often the kindest and apparently most loving of husbands have sinister sexual needs.

In a way it says a lot for your own loving and giving nature that he feels he can fulfil these dark needs with you.

Many men with similar desires keep them secret from the women they love, preferring to seek their gratification from prostitutes skilled in these black arts.

Do you wish he'd pay a professional to perform the acts he

commits with you? Or does that thought make you shudder with revulsion?

Some wives have actually admitted to me they don't care where or how or who their husbands have sex with as long as they don't have to play their dirty games.

In a sado-masochistic relationship one partner is aggressive and the other one is submissive.

You seem to me to be a very submissive girl which is why, I think, your husband assumed you'd submit to him.

But no one is compelled to agree to sexual practices that disgust or demean them. And perhaps, because you do feel so degraded, you'd be wise to leave now, while you're still young enough to find another partner.

The big question is, are you strong enough to go it alone? Or do you really need your husband as much as he needs you?

I can't help feeling you'll make every excuse to stay with him forever. And suffer the consequences for the rest of your married life.

A submissive woman like you could easily fall out of this particular frying pan into a much more dangerous fire.

Is he paying for his pain?

Dear Marje

We have been married for 18 months and until now everything has been fine.

Then one evening my husband brought home a blue video and for fun we watched it together.

I expected it to be a joke but it was disgusting. As a prelude to making love, a woman was whipping a naked man.

I thought it was perverted and I said so, but my husband got excited by it and he asked me if I would do the same for him, whip him with a belt. I refused point-blank.

Since then he's been going out alone more than usual and he's become very secretive, undressing in the dark and locking the bathroom door. But one morning I followed him into the bathroom and I noticed some welts and grazes on his back. So far, I haven't said anything to him.

Now I wonder if he's paying a prostitute to do what I won't do or maybe he has found himself a girlfriend as kinky as he is? I simply can't tolerate such behaviour.

97

Says Marje

All the evidence you have described does indeed point to the very thing you most fear. It certainly appears that your husband is paying another woman to whip him or he's found someone to do it for free.

That blue video must have released in him a masochistic need to be punished. Some men with these needs marry sadistic women who are only too happy to play the punishment game.

Don't imagine it's a new perversion invented by cynical video producers to sell their products. But it's only in recent times that a person has been able to go into a shop and buy an explicit sex video which stirs up basic instincts.

It's possible your husband might never have recognised this instinct if it hadn't been stimulated by the film. It would be very difficult for someone like yourself, who shudders with justifiable disgust, to be able to understand and accept your husband's need.

But I doubt if he will now give up this newfound pleasure. How can you tackle this unsettling problem? You can begin by telling your husband you have seen for yourself the evidence of what's going on. Ask him about his mysterious comings and goings. Ask why he now undresses in the dark, why he's trying to conceal the truth. He'll find it difficult to refute the evidence. But when it's out in the open, what then?

You might extract a promise from him to stop but I doubt if he'll be able to keep that promise. The question is, can you live with it? This question is a very tough one for you to answer.

In the end, perhaps, the strength of your love will help you to decide. But it won't necessarily help you to cope.

Sadly, unless your husband does abandon his new "hobby", you'll either have to join him or leave him. There really are no other options.

Put off my sick sex

Dear Marje

My boyfriend and I have lived happily together for two

years and we're thinking about getting married. A month ago, his best friend did just that – and the trouble started with the stagnight.

The men went on some kind of a hoolie which included a blue movie. My boyfriend came home the worse for wear and started doing some of the things he'd seen on the screen. I can't even describe the revolting practices he wanted to do.

Luckily he passed out and I thought it was just the drink getting to him. But now he's sober and he knows what he's doing and what he wants of me.

And he says if I refuse to be degraded and to degrade him, he'll leave me for someone who doesn't think sex is dirty. I love him and want him the way he was, but not the way he is now. Could it, do you think, just be a phase he'll grow tired of?

Says Marje

It could be, but who knows? I suspect, though, that now he's developed a taste for the sexual practices you have no words to describe, your boyfriend will continue to demand them. You say he wants to degrade you and I can guess what those practices are.

They are to do with the bodily functions usually performed alone in the privacy of the bathroom or the loo. Am I right? I know I am. I can read all too easily between the lines of your letter.

Your boyfriend might, if he's lucky, find a woman prepared to oblige him. Some would readily do so and I suppose anything goes if both parties are willing.

I am no prude and I don't make moral judgments, but to my mind a man who demands sexual degradation as the price of love will also degrade his partner in every other aspect of their relationship and throughout their lives together.

People who think that sex is dirty are, indeed, pathetic creatures and sex isn't dirty if people engage in practices designed to give each other mutual pleasure and fulfilment.

Note, please, the words "each other". The basis of good sex is the willingness to give and receive enjoyment.

Once one partner starts on the kind of route your boyfriend

has taken, there's positively no hope for a future with him – not for you. Not for a woman who is as disgusted as you are by his filthy demands. You claim to love him, but I think you love the man he was, not the man he now is and you are never going to be able to turn back the clock.

Let him go to find his dirty sex. I think it might take time for you to feel clean again as well as to get over your loss.

He's no loss really. When you can come to terms with that, you'll feel fresher than a daisy.

A sex line addict's sad hang-up

Dear Marje

As a 37-year-old bachelor I am a very lonely man. I have no social life. I hate pubs, because I am shy and find it hard to mix with people.

While thumbing through a paper I noticed an ad giving details of a sex chat line and I called and spoke to a girl named Mirabel.

We talked for about 30 minutes. She sounded like a lovely warm person and she told me how to reach her again and that was the start of my secret sex life.

It went on for months. We spoke for hours and she was much more to me than a disembodied voice and I fell in love with her.

I tried to make a date with her but she said it was against the rules to meet a punter. I got sexual relief by listening to her telling me what to do.

When the phone bill came I was horrified. But the worst thing of all is I've been told she has left. I long to find her. Is there anything I can do?

Says Marje

I truly hate to have to pull the plug on your romance with Mirabel but I'm afraid you're just another punter who has been conned into parting with large sums of money, and no hope of getting value for it. I suppose you did get something out of this con.

Your long, sexy chats released some of your inhibitions,

stimulating you to masturbation which gave you some relief. But for the price of a girlie mag, you could have got the same effect and a lot more cheaply.

The sad thing about all this is that you fell in love with someone who doesn't exist, except in your imagination.

You can be sure Mirabel was not the real name of the woman at the end of your hot-line. More likely Ethel, perhaps, or Gwen or Gladys (with apologies to ladies with these nice, plain names). And I don't know how you visualised her as she murmured breathlessly into your ear, but whether you saw her as a young blonde or a sultry dark-haired siren, you can be sure you got it wrong.

Chances are she was a homely middle-aged matron.

Most of the women at the end of these phone lines are ordinary females earning a living. It's safer and easier for them than going on the streets. Their job is to encourage punters like you to spend a lot of money on phone calls.

The company they work for gets a percentage of the profits. I regard it as a particularly obscene trade because so many of the punters are lonely, sex-starved men, particularly vulnerable to the filth they pay good money to buy.

You must give up your search for Mirabel, who has probably changed her name to Christabel or Manuela or something which sounds equally exotic. The more exotic the name, the more erotic the dialogue to lure the punter into greater and greater expense.

Write to me again, please, telling me where I can send you my leaflet about how to cope with shyness. It's free. I don't even want a SAE. All I want is for you to be able to join the human race and hang up on that phone-line forever.

She can't forgive her pervert husband

Dear Marje

A few weeks ago my husband and I went to a party and I got seriously drunk. My husband had to put me to bed and then we started to make love.

As we were staying the night with relatives I told him to

stop in case we made a noise, but he wouldn't and frankly I was too drunk to protest.

Then he performed perverted sex acts on me. I would have had to shout to make him stop, so I kept quiet. He had tried it once before and I hated it. It was as though I was being raped.

I feel I can never forgive him, that I will never trust him again, and I cringe every time he touches me.

I do want my marriage to survive, and I still want to stay with him, but I can't get over the fact that he abused me when I couldn't look after myself.

Now I feel dirty and used, and like it was my own fault. I am also sleeping badly. I need your help, please.

Says Marje

That feeling of being used and dirty is the way most women who are raped describe their reaction. They also, most of them, feel that they were responsible for what happened to them. It's extraordinary that a victim of crime should feel it was all somehow her fault.

I suppose, to be fair to your husband, you let him get away with it once and, if he thought at all, he'd have assumed you'd have no objection if he repeated his nasty performance.

It also occurs to me that he might have had a few drinks too many as well, and was therefore not entirely responsible for what happened that night.

But I'm not making excuses for him. No woman is forced to endure such humiliation and fear.

Rape, though, is a tricky issue. Whether or not he actually raped you is questionable.

You may have said: "Hush, don't make so much noise", but you admit you were too drunk to make a real protest.

I wish you'd been a bit more specific about the sex you describe as "perverted".

Some women think that oral or anal sex is a perversion. Others go along happily with men who enjoy it. But whatever it was, you hated it and there's no rule which says you have to put up with it.

Because you can neither forgive nor trust him, what's the point of trying to keep such an unhappy marriage together? Why do you still want to stay with him? Maybe you are scared of coping with life on your own. But how can you face the years ahead with a man who frightens you and abuses you? You could issue him with an ultimatum, demanding a promise of decent, considerate behaviour, but ultimatums rarely work and promises are easily broken in the heat of the moment and the height of passion.

Leave him – or accept the risk that it'll probably happen again and yet again.

And I'm afraid you will only have yourself to blame if it does.

Sex slave to a monster

Dear Marje

The story of my life is horrendous. My parents used drugs and there was a lot of violence between them.

When I was 13 my father raped me. He did it again and again but my mother didn't want to know.

I ran away and at 14 became a street prostitute. One of my clients was an older man who was very kind to me, and I gave up soliciting for his sake.

When I was 16, we got married and for a few years I was happy and secure for the first time in my life. I had a son, then a daughter. It was after the birth of the second baby that history began to repeat itself.

My husband doesn't use drugs but he sexually abuses and rapes me. I also have to go in for unnatural sex acts while his friend watches and sometimes joins in.

I am afraid to leave him, there are the children and where could I go? I have no money and no way of earning any, except the old way. I couldn't bear to go back to that.

I want my kids to grow up respecting me. Please can you help me?

Says Marje

Of all the awful stories people have told me, yours is one of the most horrific.

Violence, drugs and rape were part of everyday family life. Some family life. How you've survived is beyond me. The man you married, whom you assumed would protect you, is as flawed as were your parents.

I suspect your attraction for him at the beginning was your extreme youth. He didn't want a mature woman. He wanted a child he could violate and control. One, he no doubt figured, sufficiently street-wise sexually to be able to satisfy his lust. I'm surprised he married you. Perhaps he loved you while you were still a child and now he's punishing you – literally – for growing up.

I know one thing – you must do what you did when your father's abuse became too much for you to take.

You must run away yet again. Only this time you'll have your children with you.

Your husband's rape and the unnatural practices are criminal offences. The police could investigate and take action if appropriate. I hope you won't be too scared to contact them.

From what you've told me, I think they would. I know how frightened you are for your life and for the children.

You must leave this monster before history repeats itself in an even more sinister form. Your children could be at risk from sexual assault by their father.

If you go to the library, you can find out how to see a social worker who should be able to help you. You could go to the Citizens Advice Bureau, whose address you can get from the library.

For temporary shelter, do please phone the Women's Aid Federation Helpline on 0272 633542. This line is open from 10am to 4pm Monday to Friday.

I strongly urge you to get away before your children's lives are as threatened as yours was and, I fear, still is.

Sex for a living is no fun

Dear Marje

I have decided to become a prostitute and would appreciate some advice how to go about it.

Perhaps I ought to explain why I have come to this decision.

I got married at 18 but it didn't work out. We just weren't suited and he started having affairs. He left me

after five years and I divorced him. Then I lived with a man for another five years and he also walked out on me. I hated both of them. They were pigs. In fact I've never met a man I liked. Even my father is a pig who knocks my mother about. I have been out of work for two years. I can't find a job and I'm broke. I've heard that prostitutes make a good living and I don't mind sex as long as I don't have to do it with the same man every night.

I expect you've had experience concerning this profession and could give me some idea about getting started. I live in a port so there shouldn't be any shortage of clients. Thanks in advance.

Says Marje

You're welcome, although I don't think you'll be offering me any thanks when I pass on information about the profession you wish to enter. Soliciting is illegal and will land you in trouble with the law. It is dangerous and often unbelievably disgusting. You cannot pick and choose your customers.

I have it straight from a judge that it will cost you a fair slice of your takings when you are picked up for soliciting.

For a first-time offender, I understand the fine is likely to be anything from £25 to £50. It could rise to £150 or more next time, and even to as much as £1,000.

But there are consequences more costly than money – like risk to life and health. Many girls who ply their trade on the street pick up sexually transmitted diseases.

Many clients demand horrible sexual practices. When paying for such services, the punter expects value for his money. And you could get the same kind of violence from your clients that your mother gets from father. I'm not suggesting that every man who buys sex from a prostitute is a diseased, perverted brute. On the contrary, many men seek quick relief, pay and slip away into the night.

Before you put on the fishnet tights and stiletto heels, remember you'll be better off and safer on Social Security.

I think you have a romantic image of prostitution. Believe me, there's nothing romantic about it. Perhaps you think it's one way of demonstrating your hatred of men. It's much more likely that most of the men who'll use you will be demonstrating their hatred of women.

105

WHICH SIDE AM I ON?

Gay son's family torment

Dear Marje

I am 26 and I am gay. I have come to accept it and I have made no attempt to hide it.

I came out a couple of years ago and I spend a lot of time in gay clubs and pubs. I have gay friends, too, but no one special at the time of writing.

The problem is that my family can't accept the way I am. My mother and brothers treat me like I'm a misfit. They can't understand that I'm different. My brothers love women and they take every opportunity to jeer at me.

Recently my mother walked into my room when I was reading some explicit gay magazines and she went spare. She called me every kind of filthy name and she threatened to call the police.

Now she's started opening my mail and she has destroyed all the gay mags. Is it wrong to show your feelings if you're homosexual? I respect my brothers' preferences. Why can't my family respect mine?

Dear Marje

It's great that you don't try to live a lie. And why should you? But it's hardly any wonder that many gays feel compelled to do just that when they come up against the prejudices in today's society.

It is sad for you that your mother and brothers share those prejudices, but they are no different from countless families who can't understand that being gay doesn't mean you're a freak.

I've had numerous letters from parents who ask for help in trying to understand gay children – daughters as well as sons – but your mother is the first I've come across who actually threatened to call the police to shop her gay son for reading naughty magazines.

I shake my head in wonderment. If a man's own family react

this way to their gay son, what chance does he have in the tough outside world?

But while I deplore your mother's reaction and your brothers' sneering jibes, I think that you are as guilty of failure to understand as they are.

You can't see, can you, that the lifestyle you have adopted is completely foreign to them? I daresay your mother hoped all her boys would marry and have children and make her a gran.

Her anger with you is a demonstration of her bitter disappointment. You must try to be more tolerant towards your family than they are towards you.

Many parents of homosexual offspring have been helped by the organisation Acceptance, 64 Holmside Avenue, Halfway Houses, Sheerness, Kent ME12 3EY. They ask for an A5 SAE. They run a telephone helpline on 0795 661463 Tuesday-Friday 7pm to 9pm.

If only your mother would contact Acceptance, life could be easier for you all. Mean while, I hope that since you wrote to me you have found that special someone.

A husband's visit sparks gay fear

Dear Marje

I am living a nightmare. At 59, after 30 years of marriage, I think my husband, now 65, has become a homosexual.

We have three grown-up children and five grandchildren and, although we have never talked about such things, our married life has always been quite normal.

I have done my duty and been a good wife and, to give him credit, he has been a reasonably good husband, too. But over the past few months he has become very close to another man about his own age, a bachelor he visits every evening.

A neighbour told me she's noticed that sometimes the man's bedroom light is on. My husband says they play chess! It all seems very unnatural to me. He's sometimes told me lies, so there's no point in confronting him, though I'd be much too embarrassed to raise the subject. I would be grateful for your comments, please.

107

Says Marje

You have offered me an open invitation to have a real go at you but I won't. I don't want to hurt you. But I would like you to pull yourself together and try to take a sensible view of your marriage and your old man.

I'd strongly advise you to take a long hard look at the nosy neighbour who seems to have taken upon herself the role of the neighbourhood spy. She's been watching too many nail-biting spy mysteries on the telly, I reckon.

Or else she's so bored with her own life, she enjoys stirring up a bit of trouble in other people's lives. Yours, for one.

Perhaps your husband, too, has been pretty bored, without you ever realising it. While you were busy rearing the family and faithfully performing your matrimonial duties, he might well have been secretly yearning for the even greater excitement and fulfilment of a good game of chess.

And meeting this other old boy has at least given him the chance to make his dreams come true. No one, of course, could guarantee that they don't play any other games together.

Only if your kindly neighbour was able to get a close-up view of what they get up to through a chink in the curtains, could you possibly know if your suspicions were justified.

But I'd take a bet that those suspicions are totally unfounded. It's very sad that you grew up in an age when few couples could talk to each other frankly about sex.

Ideally, you should be able to say to your spouse, "You don't by any chance, happen to fancy old so-and-so, do you?" Whereupon, he'd laugh his head off.

There's altogether too much unhealthy suspicion in your marriage. As for a few porkies your husband may have told you now and then, I daresay you've told him a few too.

Forget all this homosexual rubbish. All the poor man wants is a nice game of chess and a bit of peace and quiet. End of comments. I hope they've helped.

Scared of sex with his wife

Dear Marje

I thought my luck had changed at last when I met the woman I married last year. She was divorced, I was a bachelor. I've been a loner all my life. I had never had a proper relationship with a woman, only plenty of what you might call improper ones. I've been a very lonely man, unable to find a woman to love.

When I wanted sex I went to prostitutes and I've done things I am now deeply ashamed of. Frankly, I don't know how to make love with a decent woman like my wife.

She is very sweet and warm but I can't bring myself to love her physically. I can't even bring myself to tell her how much I love her. Her first husband was a brutal alcoholic and I desperately want to make up to her for all her past misery. I am 47 and she is a year younger and I'd be forever in your debt if you could help me.

Says Marje

One thing I have to mention before I get down to your problem. You are one among millions of men who can never bring themselves to utter the words a woman longs to hear ... "I love you".

They make jokes and use daft coded phrases, like "you're not a bad old trout then". Or "I quite fancy you when you're mad at me, you stupid sausage."

You don't , in fact, have to spell out your love to a wife like yours. She knows. What she doesn't know and doesn't need to know is that your only previous sexual experience has been with prostitutes.

I can't guess why you've found it impossible to form a relationship with ordinary women. A psychiatrist might trace the reasons back to a dominant mother or a wimpish dad. Or vice versa. Actually, I don't think it matters. What does is that you now feel so dirty about paying prostitutes for sex.

And it's this association of dirt and disgust with sex that is the cause of your inhibition.

Has it ever occurred to you that your wife might actually appreciate being a little less decent than you expect her to be? For goodness sake, as well as hers and yours, give her the chance and the encouragement to let herself go.

But don't rush her. Gradually increase the passion and I believe she'll respond.

Remember, love is a comparatively new experience for you and love has nothing to do with the way you got sexual relief in the past. You have now committed yourself to a woman you love and although you can't yet say those three vital little words, given time you will.

Get in some practice by asking her if she loves you and when she murmurs yes, say "me, too". Ungrammatical, maybe, but a start. Loving this woman who was so lucky to have found you will help to wipe out the uneasy memories of your seedy past.

Disturbed dreams of a butch lover

Dear Marje

I'm a healthy 23-year-old girl, very happy with my present boyfriend, though we are not going steady.

We often have sex and it's great, nothing kinky or weird. I like and respect him.

But recently I've been thinking a lot about a person I see once a week at a club.

She seems very masculine, with short hair, jeans and heavy boots and she has a sort of butch look I can't describe.

My secret problem is I fantasise about her making love to me.

It's ridiculous because I couldn't ever bear to kiss another girl or anything like that. I certainly don't have feelings for this girl who I hardly know. I just have these really disturbing desires.

Obviously I can't talk to anyone about it. If my friends knew they'd shun me and my boyfriend would leave me. Please tell me what's wrong with me. I am very worried.

Says Marje

You are worried aren't you, because you think you might be a lesbian.

If you were, it's no big deal and you could have a perfectly happy life with the right partner. Which goes for straights as well as gays.

But I don't think your sexual fantasies about another woman

prove you are homosexual. There is fair evidence that you aren't. There's the frequent sex with your boyfriend and your shuddering rejection of the idea, even, of kissing a girl.

But let's go back to the sex with your boyfriend. Do I detect a wistful note when you mention the "respectable" aspect of this relationship?

You emphasise that nothing kinky or weird goes on. Is there, perhaps, a vague wish that there was more excitement than there is?

I have a feeling that your attraction towards the girl in the club is a symptom of your sexual frustration.

You want your nice boyfriend to do naughty things – the things this girl does in your fantasies.

Perhaps this link hasn't occurred to you, and perhaps when you consider it, it'll make sense to you.

I wouldn't agree that your fantasies are disturbing – or they shouldn't be. They're merely the result of a feeling of dissatisfaction. The fact that you fantasise about a woman rather than a man is neither here nor there in these circumstances. Anyone to latch your restless dreams on to would do.

Countless people – both men and women – enjoy fantasies. I can reassure you that your sexy dreams are nothing to worry about.

You simply want more lusty sex. Tell your boyfriend, if you can bring yourself to. If you can't, it's as well you're not going steady.

The next one might bring you greater satisfaction as well as a more frank and open relationship.

Dilemma of a gay husband
Dear Marje

I was 22 when I got married seven years ago. My wife is a super girl, funny, attractive, loves our two sons, as I do. I suppose you've guessed that the problem is sex.

When I was at school I had a few flings with other boys, the usual things school kids do, and then I met my wife.

I realised very soon after our wedding that I was gay, but for years I repressed my needs and pretended they didn't exist though I was very attracted to men. But I resisted

111

temptation because I am a married man and a religious one. I'm not a regular churchgoer though my wife is. Now the worst has happened. I have fallen in love with another gay man. It is not just sex, though that is fantastic.

I now know what has been lacking all these years. He's begging me to leave my wife but how could I square my conscience? I must either continue to live a lie or be my true self. Can you help with my terrible dilemma?

Says Marje

Terrible it most certainly is. I am sure you must lie awake at night for hours wondering what to do – not for the best – but because there's no best solution for you.

You are, indeed, a tragic victim of your sexuality. The sad thing is that you are such a good man.

Your average selfish bastard (excuse me) of a man, wouldn't think twice about putting his own needs and desires before anyone else's. But if you leave your wife for your lover, you will be betraying not only her but your faith and your church.

Pondering your problem, it occurred to me to suggest you go and talk to your vicar or priest. But on second thoughts, what can he say to you?

I imagine he'd urge you to set aside your physical needs, renounce this man and sacrifice those needs to preserve your marriage.

That would be sound advice. I'd feel inclined to second it, except that I am thinking of the years ahead.

For now that you've had a "fantastic" sexual experience, with your lover, will you ever be able to make love again to your wife?

You can be sure you won't be able to stay in your closet forever. Whatever you decide to do in the end will spell tragedy and disaster for you and your family.

My inclination is to advise you to tell your wife the truth. She must be given the chance to rebuild her life. She's young enough to start again.

You may be surprised to learn that some women, on discovering their husbands had gay lovers, have told me they'd rather lose their men to another man than to another woman.

I wish I could see a happy ending for you. I only hope that

your faith, while not being able to solve the problem, will give you comfort and help you to come to terms with whatever decision you finally make.

Gay lover goes straight down the aisle

Dear Marje

We have had five marvellous years together, my gay partner and I. Now he has told me that he's decided to leave and try to find a wife.

He says he's tired of living a "fringe" life. He wants what he calls a "normal" family life with children. I take that to mean a boring, stultifying suburban life that would drive him mad.

He loves rave-ups and going to no-holds-barred gay clubs. I am sure his family, in particular his mother who is an interfering old bat, is behind all this. She has great influence over him and lately she's been chuntering on about how fulfilling family life is – showing off the latest snaps of the grandchildren.

It's not only for my sake that I want to make him see sense, but for his. I've got to stop him destroying both our lives.

Says Marje

Although you have a vested interest in doing everything you can to prevent your lover leaving you, I understand your panic and sympathise with you. I don't think you've any right to stop him. Nor do I think it makes sense to try to frustrate his longing to be a "normal" husband and father.

As it happens I doubt if he'll succeed. If his mother is putting pressure on him, he must be terribly torn by his feelings for you and his anxiety to do as his mummy tells him.

There seem to be few dull moments in your life together. Perhaps he's beginning to feel he'd like a more peaceful, domesticated life. But has he, I wonder, considered the price he'll pay for this?

First he must find a woman. It will be a rare one who could

take on a man who has been a homosexual all his life. If he's lucky enough to do so, he will need to have an intimate physical relationship with her in order to father children. I wonder if he's thought this "normal" family business through?

Most gays I know are very affectionate towards their women friends. But that's a world away from contemplating sexual intercourse with them.

But you do not further your cause by being so offensive about your lover's mother. You will only succeed in making him very protective towards her. My advice is to do nothing. Wish him luck and assure him of your undying love and friendship.

My bet is he'll fail to achieve his goal and then he'll come back, praying you won't have found someone else.

The lonely feeling of a cross-dresser

Dear Marje

I live alone and I'm perfectly happy with my own company. At 43, with no wife or girlfriend, I can conduct my life the way I want to. I am transvestite and when I get home from work, I change into women's clothes and relax.

One evening last week a colleague arrived unexpectedly and was shocked and horrified when he saw the way I was dressed.

I gave him a drink and tried to explain that I'm normal and still the man he knows at work. But he left very soon and he avoided me next day at the office.

Other colleagues are avoiding me too and it's obvious he's told everyone. I overheard one of the girls saying she knew I was gay. I am not a homosexual. I've had good sex with several women but I've never wanted to form a lasting relationship because a woman wouldn't be able to understand my needs. I'm now having problems coping at work. If the boss gets to know, my job might be threatened.

Says Marje

One of the reasons why life can be so tough for men like you

114

is that transvestites and gays, too, are the butt of ignorant, prejudiced jokers.

Not that it will help you much to know the reason why people fall about laughing at cross-dressers, but perhaps if you could bring yourself to pity their stupidity you'd be able to shrug off the prejudice.

In a way, it might not be a bad thing that your secret is out and it would be good if you could crack jokes about it.

The most disturbing aspect of your life is your isolation. You claim to be happy with your own company, but I wonder if you're kidding yourself.

You are certain that a woman would never understand your need or cope with it, but you are wrong. I know of many happy relationships where the woman not only accepts the situation but often goes shopping with her loved-one for his dresses and undies.

For some women the initial shock of discovery is immense, but most women who love their partners manage in time to come to terms with the situation.

You are condemning yourself unnecessarily to a life of increasing loneliness, when you should be dating women and looking for one who realises you're a nice ordinary man, looking for a loving, understanding partner.

I know that forming a lasting relationship could be tricky. Should you tell the truth from the start? I believe you should so that you both know where you are before you get too deeply involved.

As for that mob at work, ignore their stares and whispers if you can. Act the way you always do. But above all, demonstrate that you've got a sense of humour. I hope you have. And I don't think you are likely to be fired for wearing frocks out of office hours as long as you wear manly grey suits at work.

Guilt over games boys play

Dear Marje

For years I have been very uneasy about what happened between me and my best friend when we were schoolboys.

We were about seven when we started mucking about and playing rude kids' games.

We showed each other our private parts and, young as we were, we compared sizes.

We touched each other up and as we got into our teens, we masturbated each other. Then we both started taking a healthy interest in girls.

After we left school, we went our separate ways and lost touch until a couple of years ago when we met again by chance. He was living with a girl and I was engaged.

We see each other quite often but I feel awful when we meet. It stirs up all the old guilt.

I love my wife. We have great sex but this cloud hangs over me.

Sometimes I wonder if I am secretly perverted because although I've never had sex with another male, frankly I am curious about it.

I'm really mixed up and I hope you can help me.

Says Marje

You are no more mixed-up than countless other men. The main difference, though, between you and them is that you are honest enough to confront your feelings and your guilt. That's a healthy attitude.

There can't be many men who when young have never mucked about with each other behind the bike shed. Girls do it, too.

Your experiments with your school friend were as important a part of your learning process as geography and history and maths.

Those youthful playground larks prepared you for the manhood you are now enjoying. Or would be enjoying if it wasn't for the unnecessary guilt you still feel.

Many heterosexual men have a passing curiosity about homosexuality, and that isn't such a bad thing. It compels you to make choices.

You made yours many years ago when you began to pursue women and married the one you love.

I think you were lucky to meet your old friend again, despite the feelings you describe. You feel awful because you are ashamed of those youthful fumblings. If you could be as frank with each other now as you were when you were schoolboys, I guarantee he'd confess to similar guilt.

It's interesting that comparing size has always been a male obsession. A perfectly harmless one, in my view.

It's like the way women compare breast sizes and it's simply because penises and breasts are symbols of sexuality and performance. You are performing OK. You'd get 10 out of 10 and a gold star, I bet, from a wife who is satisfied her husband is all man.

I hope my observations will help to lift that cloud.

Why don't you fix up a foursome dinner date with your pal and his girl and drink a toast to the good old days, the days that changed you from a boy into a manly man? I'll drink to that with you.

Teacher's pet

Dear Marje

At school I always felt different from the other girls, especially when they went on and on about boyfriends. When I was about 16, my parents split up and I got very depressed and my school work suffered.

But I had a kind and sympathetic teacher. She began inviting me to her home and she helped me with my work. But she also taught me more than I'd bargained for.

Before long she was making love to me although I knew it was wrong. It went on for about a year, when she left for another job.

I am now 22. I have never had a relationship with a man. I am a lesbian. Sometimes I go to to gay pubs and clubs and I have a few gay friends but no one special.

I feel I am a misfit and I'll never forgive that teacher who sexually abused me and abused my trust and made it impossible for me to lead a normal, happy life. I don't suppose there's any way you can help me.

Says Marje

I'm not clear in my mind if you blame the teacher for the fact that you are a lesbian. If you do, you do her an injustice, although she certainly did more homework with you than was necessary for your education.

I think you, yourself, while holding her responsible, have nagging doubts. You admit you yawned with boredom when the other girls at school banged on about boyfriends and all that stuff – but you freely acknowledge that you've never wanted a man and you acknowledge, too, your lesbianism.

What puzzles me is why you are so convinced you are a misfit. I don't go along with that assessment. Depressed, yes. Lonely, certainly. But at 22 you're one of many girls who haven't yet found a partner with whom you can make a loving commitment.

I think you are grabbing at the break-up of your parents' marriage to label yourself a victim. True, children are always the victims of broken marriages but you weren't a confused toddler.

You were an adolescent who had a fair grasp of the situation and although it was tough for you, I think you are using the break-up as an excuse for adopting the lesbian lifestyle you feel you should have rejected.

But it's clear that with or without the bust-up, and whether or not you'd been seduced by the teacher, you are gay. So why not accept it and enjoy it?

If that teacher hadn't initiated you in the joy of sex, some other woman would have and it's nothing either to be ashamed of or to boast about. It's like having green or brown eyes. You can't change them. But you can see the world with them.

Continue to go where you'll meet others like yourself and there's a very good chance indeed that one day you'll meet your soul-mate.

Just stop apologising to yourself for what you are and, like every other hopeful 22-year old girl, you'll soon start to lead the happy life which, like all of us, you yearn to have.

A gay girl strays

Dear Marje

I felt a lot of anguish before I could accept I was a lesbian. At 25, I fell in love and she and I lived very happily

together for six years. Our love was based on trust as well as sex and friendship. A few weeks ago when I was looking for our car keys I came across some condoms in her handbag. I asked her for an explanation and she admitted she was having sex with a colleague at work, the first man she'd ever been with.

She wept and said she knew she'd been a fool and promised to stop going with him. She said she did it out of curiosity. But I left her and am now back living with my disapproving parents. My mother is particularly hard – always has been.

My girlfriend has bombarded me with letters and phone calls begging me to go back. But it's obvious she must be bisexual and though I'm terribly tempted because I still love her, wouldn't she be likely to betray me again? I couldn't go through any more heartbreak.

Says Marje

You may be convinced your girlfriend is bisexual, but I am not so sure. I think there's probably some truth in her explanation that she wanted to have sex with a man out of curiosity. Perhaps she has never been quite so certain about her sexuality as you are about yours.

It's pretty plain you lacked love and warmth during your formative years. I'm sure you've always felt a desperate yearning for your mother's love – a love that was never forthcoming.

It wasn't until you met your friend that you knew what a woman's love and tenderness meant.

Don't condemn her for trying to sort out her sexual needs. Having experimented with a man, she now realises what she really wants, which is you.

Not only for sex, but for everything you shared – the friendship and companionship and the mutual comfort of facing together a world which is often very hostile to lesbian women.

I realise you now feel the trust you shared has been eroded, that you can never again rely on her fidelity. But I wonder if she will always be able to rely on yours?

I'm not suggesting you'd ever be tempted to shop for condoms and get a man to try them for size, but you might fall

119

in love with another woman. Relationships don't come with a written guarantee that they'll last forever. I can't tell you whether or not she'd betray you again or whether you'll ever betray her. Lovers have to take a chance and learn that forgiveness and charity are two of the essential ingredients of love.

If you do go back to your friend, I hope you'll both have learned useful lessons which should make your partnership even stronger in the future.

EXCUSES, EXCUSES

Door-to-door lust is driving him berserk

Dear Marje

I'm an insurance rep, calling from door-to-door to make collections. I meet plenty of women on my rounds.

And although I'm not particularly good-looking, I get offers galore and a lot of pressure from my clients.

Although I am happily married, I find it impossible not to give in. There are so many women who want a bit of excitement in their lives.

Over the last few years I have had numerous affairs but I know that I won't be able to get away with it forever.

Sooner or later my wife's going to find out. Or one of their husbands will.

What can I do to curb my sexual appetite?

Says Marje

Poor you. It's a tough life, selling insurance and chucking in your sexual favours as a bonus. Your trouble is you're too good natured, a benefactor for sex-starved womankind, performing a splendid public service.

I can picture you taking a pleading woman client by the hand to the bedroom, murmuring "There, there, duckie, you'll soon feel better" and collecting the insurance money on the way out. I'm sure you feel genuinely sorry for these ladies in need and I dare say they are very grateful for the service you provide.

You can discount any risk to them. I expect they're careful to lock the front door.

You aren't in much danger either, unless you're no longer quite up to performing this worthwhile service for your wife, when she might wonder why. Could you be beginning to feel pangs of conscience? As you say, you have a lot to lose if your wife found out, like your job, as well as her.

Now, it seems, the time has come to curb your generosity

and the bonking. Charity must begin and end – at home. It's true there will be a lot of disappointed clients and you might have to invent a convincing doorstep patter and and steel yourself for possible denunciation, like: "What's come over you then, mid-life crisis?" As a matter of fact, that's not a bad excuse. It's becoming a popular line with greying men who aren't quite as virile as they once were.

And if you suffer some discomfort at having to restrain your good works, ask the doctor for something to calm you down. That will be excellent insurance for all concerned.

Wife's a bore for randy stud

Dear Marje

We fell in love at school. We lived on the same estate and when she was 18, we got married. She was a pretty, shy blonde. In her eyes I was a handsome stud.

We've been married 12 years. We still live on the estate, with two children now, but I am going crazy with the boredom of it all.

Where once she was pretty, she is now plump, the blonde hair is brassy and dyed. There is nothing between her ears. She thinks John Major is ever so nice, she likes his glasses, for God's sake.

I suppose you can guess why I'm writing this. The other woman is a classic contrast to my wife. Six years older than me, great body, black hair, sexy as hell. The affair began a few months ago and I'm hooked.

At first she was satisfied just to make love but now she wants me to leave my wife. Usually you urge people to try to preserve their marriages but don't you agree I've a good case for cutting adrift from mine?

Says Marje

You have undoubtedly made a case, but I am not the judge and jury designated to pronounce you innocent or guilty. I usually come down on the side of the law and order of marriage, because a besotted man or woman in love with someone else is unable to see clearly the consequences of a

122

parting. I am on your side when I say to you hang on there and think this thing through. For all I know, your dark-haired love might bring you everlasting happiness. But by your own admission it seems the affair was based only on sex.

You describe her black hair and great body but do not mention any great intellectual power. What's her view, if any, of Mr Major and his glasses?

Do you chat about the ERM and the faltering economy as you rest between sessions of panting passion?

I put these questions to you hoping they'll help to clarify a mind clouded by being on a permanent sexual high. You know as well as I do that as time goes by the passion inevitably fades.

Fair enough. It's all the other elements you have to consider, whether it is, in fact, a meeting of minds as well as of genitals.

Whether this fiery woman would keep the boredom at bay. Whether life with her would be so tempestuous that you'd long for the peace of boredom.

You have to weigh every pro against every con. I haven't mentioned your children and you referred to them only in passing.

Whether or not their loss would break your heart is another pro or con to weigh.

I'm sorry I can't say to hell with everything, love – or sex – is all. I know it isn't.

Those two enemies of contentment, guilt and regret, will always be around to haunt you should you decide to bid your childhood sweetheart goodbye.

He fancies his lover's daughter

Dear Marje

When I met the woman I'm living with, the age gap – I'm 25 and she's 20 years older – didn't matter. We'd both broken up from previous long-lasting relationships and we needed each other for sex, which was very good, and for companionship.

But the passion is cooling, and I'm tremendously attracted to my lover's lovely 18-year-old daughter. She's very like her mother but her mother has put on weight and

123

I am aware now of the wrinkles and stretch marks I never noticed before.

The woman and I have lived together for about a year and I don't want to hurt her but I do want her daughter. I know it's a very difficult problem and I'd be grateful for your help in solving it.

Says Marje

Presumably, the girl you fancy also fancies you. Or are you simply fantasising about her? Make up your mind about that before you abandon the mother for the daughter.

You must also be confident that the daughter would be prepared to cause her mother the pain and humiliation your defection would mean.

There is another little matter you must take on board. The girl won't remain flawless forever. She, too, will get wrinkles and probably put on weight.

If she bears children, she, too will very likely get stretch marks, along with wet nappies, bags under the eyes and all the other joys of motherhood.

Or will you look around for another ravishing young girl when this one enters her fading forties?

And here's another question: What will you yourself look like at 40? Will you still be trim and sexy – or will you have started to creep over the hill – with a bit of a beer belly and the somewhat limp sexual equipment that all too often goes with it?

Examine your motives before you take a step you might always regret. If you can honestly say you no longer love your lady, gently tell her so and then move out.

Don't, I beg you, tell her you are considering inviting her daughter to step into Mum's shoes or knickers or whatever.

Put the budding relationship with the girl on the back burner for the time being and keep the flame very low. There's no point in causing more hurt than is necessary to someone you once loved. It'll be hard enough on her to lose you, but devastating to lose you to her own child.

I hope that when you go, as I'm sure you plan to, she'll soon find another man to console her. A grown-up one, preferably, not another selfish toyboy.

HAPPY ENDINGS

Flirty husband is just a big joke

Dear Marje

It was obvious from the start that my husband had a roving eye. He couldn't resist gazing meaningfully at every attractive girl he met.

At first I had terrible misgivings about marrying him. He even made a mild pass at my sister, who warned me he'd break my heart. But I was madly in love and despite all the chatting up of other girls, I knew he loved me.

But even on our honeymoon he was calling out to girls in scanty swimsuits on the beach while snogging with me lying beside him. Luckily I've got a sense of humour and I didn't really ever feel threatened by all the gorgeous girls.

Early on in my marriage I decided to use the "if you can't beat 'em, join 'em" method. I'd point girls out to him, telling him to take a good look at large boobs, nice bottoms, long legs, etc. And it worked. He'd laugh his head off – we'd laugh together.

We've just celebrated our twenty-first year of wedded bliss, still laughing. Just thought you'd like to know.

Says Marje

Yours is the sort of letter I appreciate on a sunless morning when I know I'll be faced with a stack of letters from depressed women who, like you, are in love with men with roving eyes.

Your sense of humour has saved your marriage but it is very difficult indeed to invent a sense of humour if you don't have one. The nearest you can get is to pretend you've got one, but the laughter can be somewhat hollow unless it comes straight from the belly.

I suspect that along with your priceless ability to laugh off your old man's keen anatomical interest in other women, you

125

have a very sharp intelligence and I hope that doesn't sound patronising. It isn't meant to. I say it admiringly to a wise woman who, spotting her man's weakness early on, did some clear thinking and calmly worked out her battle plan for the survival of the relationship.

A less wise wife would have launched herself on a career of constant and persistent nagging and reproach until the man, in desperation, grabbed the first set of great boobs and long legs he could get his paws on and departed from the matrimonial home.

I have no doubt there have been times in your marriage when you've wondered how much longer you could continue to play the emotionally draining game, but you've proved it was worth keeping the laughter and the banter going.

What you did so brilliantly was remove any trace of illicit excitement or guilt from your husband's actions.

I'm sad there aren't more women like you with such a finely honed sense of humour. I wish you and your mischievous spouse many more laughing happy years together and I'm sure you'll still both be laughing when you chalk up fifty golden years.

Merry widow on a manhunt

Dear Marje

For years I put up with every kind of abuse from my husband. As well as physical cruelty and obscene sexual demands, he spoke to me like I was a dog. A dog would have got better treatment.

I endured it all because I had two children. Oh yes, he was very clever at concealing what he did. To our family and friends, he was the perfect gentleman. As for me, I hid the bruises and the scars, both physical and mental.

Sometimes I was so afraid of him, I'd lock myself in the bathroom for the night. Then, last year, he died and I rejoiced. I am now 57 and a new woman. Everyone says I look years younger. I've spent some of the money he left on my hair and clothes and recently I met a man on a cruise I treated myself to. My children condemn me for

being heartless, but I don't give a damn. I'm out to get this nice, kind man. Please Marje, wish me luck.

Says Marje

I started wishing you luck even before you asked me to. If ever a woman needed it and deserved it, you do. And the nice man will be even luckier if he gets you.

You are a spunky lady. You will, I guess, have to put up with quite a lot of flak from all the people your late unlamented husband managed to deceive. Actually, although it's no comfort or consolation to you, many husbands who are violent in the privacy of the bedroom appear to outsiders to be the soul of courtesy and charm.

What saddens me in your case – and in so many similar cases I've come across – is that the children mothers protect from the obscenities of their fathers all too often fail to give those mothers loyalty and support.

If your children had known you'd spent nights of terror locked in the bathroom to avoid their father's violence, perhaps they'd be kinder to you now. You are right to make a new life. Hopefully, that cruise will mean a new start.

I do not subscribe to the convention that it's wrong to speak ill of the dead. The fact that your husband is now departed doesn't suddenly turn this rotten character into a saint. You are entitled not to mourn him, nor need you feel guilty because you're glad he's gone.

I am glad for you. Your children should be, too. Or they surely would be if they knew the truth. And go easy with this new man. Don't scare the pants off him by chasing him. The pants will come off in good time, if you're patient.

And please do drop me another line if all my good luck prayers for you are answered. I'm a real sucker for a romantic happy ending for someone like you who deserves it.

Niggling doubts of a knicker lover

Dear Marje

When my wife of 20 years asked me what I would like for my birthday, I pointed to a magazine advert showing a girl

127

in sexy underwear and said, "those". And then I confessed to her that for years I have had fantasies about wearing women's underwear.

Imagine my surprise when, singing "Happy Birthday", she handed me a pack of three beautiful satin camiknickers. I was delighted and now I wear them most of the time.

But while I can't believe my wife has been so understanding and I wish more women were like her, I do have a niggling doubt that there's something wrong with all this.

Is it unmanly? Is there some dark sinister reason why my wife enjoys seeing me dressed in feminine underwear? Or why I should want to? Or should I just stop trying to understand it and enjoy myself?

Our sex life is better than it has ever been. I am confident and relaxed and so is she. I suppose I'm looking for reassurance that there's no harm in it.

Says Marje

I am happy to reassure you. And I, too, wish there were more women like your wife, able to accept that their transvestite partners are not perverts.

Is your need to wear women's undies unmanly, you ask. I don't know what virtue there is, if any, in being manly.

Soccer hooligans and thugs who beat up old ladies no doubt regard themselves as manly. As do men who regularly rape and hit the women in their lives.

A lot of females are under the often false impression that every well-oiled muscle-bound six footer with huge biceps and chests as big as a well-endowed women's breasts, is manly. You, enjoying great uninhibited sex with your willing wife, seem perfectly manly to me, as clearly you do to her.

I don't believe there's anything sinister about your wife's excitement when you wear your silky slinkies.

She can see for herself the excitement they engender in you and she responds to it readily, which is nice for both of you. And my advice to you is don't knock it and don't question it.

Cross-dressing is only a problem in a relationship where a transvestite partner shrinks with disgust and horror at the discovery of what her man wears under his jacket and pants.

Many men with similar needs to yours go to great lengths to try to hide the truth from wives less understanding and tolerant than yours.

Personally, I've never found it odd that some men feel good in clothes that could be described as feminine. Monks wear robes. So do priests. Knights of the Garter wear robes along with their garters.

Whether any of them wears knickers underneath is not known. But what if they do? If they're all upright men and true, good luck to them, whatever they wear in public or in private.

Carry on enjoying your happy married life and long, long may it last.

PROBLEMS, PROBLEMS

Should he seek his lost love?

Dear Marje

It was 30 years ago when I fell in love for the first time. We were 18 and we were both virgins. We had a passionate affair that lasted for about a year.

But I was a jealous, suspicious idiot. She'd only to smile at another man and I'd accuse her of wanting him. Not surprisingly, she got fed up and ended the relationship.

But at 20 I fell in love again with the woman I married. I lost touch with the first girl but friends told me that she, too, had married.

Yet even though I was very happy with my wife, I still felt pangs of jealousy when I thought about "my girl" having sex with someone else.

Two years ago my wife died and I began to think about my first love again. I made enquiries and I found out where she lives.

It appears she's divorced, with one daughter. You know what I'm thinking about don't you? Should I, or shouldn't I? And if not, why not?

Says Marje

You seem to be assuming I'll say no, don't seek out your first love. I'm not going to, but there are a few observations I must make.

You are a romantic man, believing that true love never dies and convinced your first girl would fall into your arms the moment she saw you again crying: "I've never stopped loving you either ..." It's possible but, I fear, improbable.

You have cherished, for 29 years, an image of a teenage girl. In your mind, she has never changed, never grown up, never become the middle-aged women she is now. She remains the virgin she was at 18.

In fact, she is now nearly 50. She may be a plump, cosy housewife. On the other hand, she could be a smart, high achiever in business or in a profession. Whatever she's become, it's a far cry from your tender first love.

Likewise, you are not the man you were at 18. A glance in the mirror will show you how much you've changed.

Perhaps there's a paunch where once there was a trim waist, or a balding head where once there was a thick thatch of hair. I'm sure I needn't go on.

What I'm saying is that if you do knock on that door, let your expectations be realistic. And be prepared for her to say: "I put you out of my life years ago and forgot all about you. Sorry."

She might recall those jealous scenes and shudder as she shuts her door on your retreating back.

But if, despite my reservations, you still want to contact her, write first. Be cautious, though. Say how nice it would be to meet again, for old times' sake. No lovey-dovey stuff. She might be living with a jealous man.

I have known cases where one-time lovers have met up and fallen in love again in middle and even old age.

Such cases are rare. But love, if you're lucky second time around, can be even more magical than it was the first time. You'll have both learnt useful lessons.

Is tarot leading her to Mr Wrong?

Dear Marje

About a year ago I had a tarot reading. It was really accurate about my past life and I was told that I'd meet someone who worked in a hospital – a doctor or a male nurse – and we would fall in love and marry.

Since then I've been on the lookout for a medical man. I hang around outside the local hospitals but although I have met a few nice men during the year, including a builder, a computer programmer and a salesman, I am scared about getting too close to anyone.

Suppose I made a commitment with one of these men, even got married and then too late, met the man the tarot reading told me is waiting for me somewhere? What worries me is that the reading about my past was so spot on. I am 23 and admit I'm superstitious. Do you believe in tarot readings? Do you think I can be confident that I will meet the right man?

Says Marje

You can be pretty confident you will meet your Mr Right but I think it's highly unlikely you will meet Dr Right or Mr Male-Nurse Right.

Indeed I am convinced that people who direct their lives according to the reading of tarot cards are pretty well out of their tiny minds.

I dare say I will now be positively pelted with letters from readers telling me I'm out of mine. No matter. I stick to my anti-tarot guns.

Unlike you, I am not superstitious. I do not believe my fate will be sealed if I encounter a black cat, unless I trip over it and break a leg, God forbid.

People who claim to tell fortunes or foresee the future are, I'm sure, decent honest citizens who believe they have occult skills.

For my part, I'd just as soon believe in fairies, but certainly there are people like yourself – vulnerable, anxious, seeking love and romance and all that stuff – who'd believe anything if it reinforced their dreams.

A lot of females get wildly excited when they think about men in white coats with their stethoscopes dangling.

They regard these blokes as being eminently marriageable. My very serious advice to you is to stop lurking around hospitals. You might just pick up someone undesirable.

Take another look at the builder, computer programmer – a bit dull perhaps, unless you're into lap tops – and the salesman. Re-assess them all.

One of them may well be your fate. Forget about doctors and male nurses. True, you may encounter some of these. When you have a baby, perhaps, or fall over a black cat.

I fancy the builder for you, personally. It's always handy to have a man who can put up shelves in the kitchen. Overworked doctors and male nurses would probably be far too tired.

132

Slobbery kisses she misses

Dear Marje

You will probably bin this trivial letter, but I'm so heartbroken that I don't know who to turn to.

My boyfriend and I lived together for eight years. Mostly we were happy but I did start a couple of years ago to put pressure on him to get married. But he didn't want to know. He said there was need as we didn't want children.

But we had a dog we both adored. He was just a scruffy mongrel, wild and wonderful. He came into our bed every morning to wake us up with slobbery kisses.

Then three months ago, after one of our periodic rows, my boyfriend said he was packing it in and I said OK, clear out. When I got home from work he'd left, taking all his things – and our dog.

I haven't heard from him since. His parents won't tell me where he is. I've written to him at their place but he doesn't reply. He and my dog have vanished into thin air.

I miss him, but it's my dog I miss most. I expect you're disgusted with me but it's the truth. Please don't bin this letter.

Says Marje

Well I haven't, have I? It's as sad and touching as other seemingly less trivial letters I get.

It is a very honest letter from a girl who accepts her share of the responsibility for the breakdown of the relationship. And I am certainly not disgusted at your admission that you miss your beloved dog more than you miss your partner.

That scruffy mongrel gave you unconditional love and loyalty. Which is a darn sight more than you appeared to get from his co-owner, who apparently didn't give you the loyalty and love you got from your dog. It's true it could be argued that the dog had it easy. He didn't have to endure constant nagging about getting married. He didn't have to make the bed he snuggled into every evening or go out to work to earn his Pedigree Chum. He could be sure of uncritical devotion from

133

you both. If there's a small shred of comfort for you in this tragic loss, it's the certainty that your ex-partner will take good care of the dog. But there's no way you are going to get him back.

There are no custody laws in regard to pets and I am sorry to have to tell you that you must now try to understand that you have been bereaved– as much in mourning as if you'd lost a close relative or friend.

Try to take one day at a time. Allow yourself to weep, to think about that mongrel you loved and lost, to remember the good times you spent with him. And you must be thankful that he's still alive and happy somewhere.

Losing a person – and that dog was a person to you – means being grateful for their well-being, even if they're no longer with you.

I won't do anything as daft – and trivial – as suggest you get another dog. Any more than I'd say find another man, any man to fill your lonely hours. One day though, I hope you'll find both.

Terrified by his unnatural urges

Dear Marje

I am 50 and desperate. My problem is children and my overwhelming desire to fondle them. No one has the slightest idea I am like this but I need help urgently.

I'm afraid to go to my doctor because I don't want these thoughts and urges of mine to be put on his file.

But I've heard recently of a man who had a chance to be given injections to curb these unnatural and frightening desires.

Do you know where I could get hold of something which will quell this feeling that sometimes overwhelms me? I am terrified it will get out of control.

I have tried sex with women but I can't do it. I wish to God I had the courage to end my life. I realise I am perverted and a danger to children as well as to myself. Is there anything you can do to help me?

I am haunted by your terrible confession and I've been searching for some way I can help you and the several other men like you who have sent me similar pleas for help.

I have been to see my own GP about the problems faced by paedophiles like yourself.

You are a sick man. To date, I hope, I pray, you are not a criminal. Lay your hands or your sexual organs on a child and you will be.

I do not, of course, know how men with similar desires are coping, torn apart as they are by the terror of what those desires could unleash.

I do know that because paedophilia is both criminal and horrible in most people's minds, it's not easy to find help for them. Sympathy is short on the ground. The very word brings a shudder of distaste. The only national, reputable organisation I've been able to find willing to help try to prevent men like you from committing the unthinkable is the NSPCC.

Their aim is to protect the safety and welfare of children. They have told me that you could ring their Helpline on 0800 800 500 at any time of the day or night. It is a free, 24-hour service.

They will do what they can to help you and others like you who live in fear of the harm you might do to a child.

They will also do their best for those who are already molesting children and desperately want to stop. All calls are confidential.

They also strongly recommend a visit to your doctor. My GP reminded me that every patient can be assured of confidentiality.

He shook his head when I talked about the injections you mentioned. I don't have much hope for that.

You were brave when you decided to tell me about your fears, but I'm glad your lack of courage prevented you from making the ultimate escape.

Otherwise I wouldn't have had the chance to offer you and other tortured men a chance to seek the help you urgently need and, perhaps protect children in danger.

Ditched by her celebrity lover

Dear Marje

For obvious reasons, I can't tell you the name of the man I love. He is a showbiz celebrity I met at a bash.

I managed to grab his attention and he was great, really friendly. He gave me a lift home and we took it from there. He was often away so we couldn't spend a lot of time together, but he rang me frequently and once he said he loved me.

He is not married and I am desperately in love with him.

But a few weeks ago, the phone calls came less and less often.

When he did ring he made excuses about being busy and dodged the question when I asked him if he still loved me.

He has now stopped phoning altogether. I've left messages on his answering machine and called his assistant, who always says he's out. Please don't think I'm just another star-struck fan. I want him back, I ache to see him and hear his voice.

What can I do? Where did I go wrong? Please, please help me.

Says Marje

Where you went wrong was in mistaking this man's intentions. You went wrong when you mistook his passing interest for love.

You went wrong when you believed he loved you, if in fact he did actually murmur those words.

Where he went wrong was in encouraging a besotted girl to believe there was more in a casual relationship than was the case. Even celebrities are often quite human. Even household names respond to wide-eyed, unquestioning worship. Although you don't mention your age you sound like a breathless teenager, who, knocked out by a famous face, "invented" a romance on the basis of a car-ride and a few friendly meetings and phone calls.

If this seems to be a harsh summing-up of your brief fling

with fame, believe me it's not intended as a put-down. Perhaps when he was momentarily off-guard he did say "I love you". People often do, purely out of politeness. It means, in these circumstances, no more than "have a nice day". It's a pleasantry rather than a declaration of undying love.

You say that after the first ride home in his car you "took it from there", whatever that means.

I think you mean it was the start of something significant for you. But clearly it wasn't the start of anything for him.

I'm consumed with curiosity, of course, about the identity of this citizen. You won't say and quite right too. Tuck him away in your memory book and give up your efforts to contact him. And when the ache has faded, latch your dreams onto someone more attainable than your famous star.

He must be regretting that good-natured offer of a lift home, which you so sadly misinterpreted as the start of a romantic affair.

Torture after putting down her pet

Dear Marje

With all the sad letters you get, you will probably put this one in the bin but to me it's as great a sorrow as anyone could know. I had to have my beloved dog put to sleep. He was the centre of my life for 15 years – my friend, companion and protector.

I am a widow of 67. My only son lives abroad with his wife and two children and I have no other close family.

Friends, though some have been kind, don't seem to understand. They are impatient. One said: "It was only a dog, you can get another one." One of the worst things about it is that I knew he was getting ill and old, but I was afraid of high vet's bills. A friend of mine had to spend a fortune on her cat.

Now I feel I could perhaps have somehow prolonged his life. As I write this, I wonder if you are an animal lover and would realise the depth of my grief and not sneer like some of these so-called friends.

I am not sneering. My specs are misty as I read your letter and knowing what readers of this newspaper are like, there will be countless people who'll blink their eyes and gulp as they share the pain of your loss.

As it happens, yes, I am an animal lover. But that, I think, is beside the point. The point is the guilt that comes with grief.

Whenever people lose someone close through death, guilt is an over-riding factor of their mourning. They ask themselves, could I have done more? Was I selfish? Unheeding? Did I love enough and demonstrate that love?

Those are the sort of questions which plague the mind of those left behind. Your guilt centres around your failure to seek a vet's help for your beloved friend. But who knows if a vet could have added a few more weeks or months to what was a considerable life-span?

Probably not. He was a very old dog, though in your eyes, no doubt, he was still the playful puppy who gave you so much pleasure for so long. What makes it hard for you to bear is that yours was the decision to give him the final release. But it was the right decision, the best one for him. You wouldn't have wanted him to suffer and perhaps die in pain.

You must forgive yourself. Those heartless friends can't see that your dog was to you as important and as close as any human – more, perhaps, than some.

A lot of humans could learn about loyalty and gratitude from dogs, especially those unimaginative friends of yours.

Simply disregard them. You won't believe me now, but I promise you that each day your loss will become a little easier to bear. But just as you can't go shopping for a new man when you lose one, you can't shop for a new pet either.

You can only remember all the affection you gave and all the love you got in return. Please don't let unnecessary guilt spoil your happy memories.

Truth can be cruel

Dear Marje

My best friend is a prime example of mutton dressed as

lamb. She's fair, fat and 48. Her tight skirts come up to her crotch, she dyes her hair a brassy blonde and her bulges look obscene under her see-through blouses.

One night a couple of weeks ago, she came round to my place on her way to a party, done up like a dog's dinner. She asked me how she looked and I told her the truth, that she looked terrible.

I knew she'd be seeing a man she fancied at the party – she's been on the look out for someone since her divorce – and I said he'd take one look at her and scarper. I advised her to go home and change into a nice black dress.

She slammed out, furious and she hasn't spoken to me since.

My husband says he's not surprised, the way she looks is none of my business. But don't you agree with me that friends should be honest with each other – otherwise what kind of friendship is it?

Says Marje

There's a fine difference between honesty and tact. It would have been tactful to have dodged your friend's question.

You could, for example, have said she looked great – a real knockout, though the man in her gunsight might be alarmed by such glamour.

Something along those lines may have encouraged her to nip back home and tone her gear down a bit. But I'm surprised she didn't tell you to mind your own business.

You could have countered that by reminding her she asked for your opinion. But what she really wanted from you was confirmation that she looked stunning enough to knock this man for six.

As it was, you demolished her self-confidence with a few honest words. You didn't really mean to hurt her, did you? You made a darn good job though, all in the name of friendship.

Imagine how you'd feel if you got yourself up to go on a manhunt and your best friend told you the man you were after would head for the door at first sight of you. Would you give her a fond hug and thank her for warning you? Like hell you would.

I wonder what your real motives were behind all this

139

honesty. Maybe you are envious of your friend who may not have the best of taste and wouldn't get her photo in Tatler, but who clearly does her best to look stunning. There's no reason why a woman at 48 shouldn't display what she regards as her assets.

I'm right there with your husband. Has she, perhaps, ever given him the eye or a flash of the well-upholstered boobs? Just a thought, friend.

Send her a bunch of flowers and an apology for it would be a pity to lose such a lusty friend on account of a few thoughtless words. They were thoughtless, weren't they?

Mother who lost a child twice over

Dear Marje

I had a letter from an adoption society informing me the daughter I was forced to give away 25 years ago was trying to find me. I was reluctant to open up old wounds, but I agreed to see her. She was beautiful and she had two lovely little girls who I was extremely proud of.

I got them to call me Granny and they came to see me often.

Then a year ago their visits stopped. My daughter said that she was finding the travelling difficult, but I know she never told her adoptive parents about finding me. She didn't want to hurt them.

Now I am hurt, I feel devastated at losing them again.

I wonder if my daughter did this to spite me for giving her away years ago?

I don't know if I should contact her or leave her alone. Please advise me.

Says Marje

It is a sad fact that in many cases the reunion between natural parents and the children they gave up for adoption doesn't work out.

It's particularly sad because all of the parties concerned ache so much for the meeting to be a happy ending to a tragic beginning. There are offspring longing to meet their natural parents, for whom they may have searched over many years. And there are parents who have yearned to trace the children they parted from years ago.

All too often the searches end in tears and disappointment.

Your daughter looked for you because she wanted to find her roots. Natural and understandable.

But when at last you met each other you were a couple of total strangers. The only fragile tie was a tie of blood.

There was no valid relationship, no common background, no shared interest, no family love.

If you had met each other casually the chances are you might never have gone beyond a nodding acquaintance.

It's very hard for a mother like you to accept that you are your daughter's mother only in name.

Her adoptive parents are the ones she has always known as her mum and dad.

She was their beloved little girl, not yours.

You had to sacrifice your motherhood and I'm afraid that your sacrifice must continue.

I don't think your daughter backed off to spite you for giving her away when she was a baby.

I believe she did it to protect her children and out of consideration for the couple they've always known as granny and grandpa – the couple who have loved her as a daughter all her life.

Don't contact her. I know you feel devastated and bereaved and my heart goes out to you.

But when you feel better, as you will, ring up your local social services department and offer to become an "adoptive" grandparent.

A child who will never know a real nan will be forever grateful to be able to cuddle you and call you "granny".

Stepfather freezes out her son

Dear Marje

Divorced, with a 10-year-old son, I felt brilliant when I met and married my present husband.

My happiness was complete when I got pregnant five months before the wedding. Our daughter is now five years old and her father idolises her.

But he has changed beyond belief since she was born. He's no longer interested in sex. He's off-hand with me and has become hateful to my son.

At first he was a great stepdad and my son said he was his best friend. Now his stepfather rarely talks to him and when he does, it's to slag him off.

The other day my husband actually told him to clear out for good.

My boy now spends hours alone in his room or he leaves the house as soon as his stepfather comes in. I don't know how to handle this terrible situation, especially as my son said last night he feels like bunking off.

Says Marje

There are a lot of confusing cross-currents in your very dodgy marriage and I think you must try to unravel them and look at each element separately.

Go right back to the beginning. Do you think, looking back, that yours could have been a shotgun wedding, that your husband married you because you were expecting his child?

Did you put any pressure on him to marry you? Or was he a man with such a strong sense of responsibility that he was determined to do the right thing?

Although some men make a bolt for it when they get a girl pregnant, there are still many who want to acknowledge paternity. I'm putting forward theories and I think you'd be sensible to consider them. They could account for his present behaviour.

Can you face the fact that he may never really have loved

you, that he tolerated your son because he had little choice, that he idolises his daughter and gives her all the love that's in him to give? The stepparent relationship is almost always tricky. Jealousy is one of the greatest causes of family quarrels.

There are conflicting loyalties, even when the marriage is a good and loving one. Which yours, sadly, no longer is.

I think that it was based on sex, not love – on his part at any rate – and you and both your children are victims of a passion that has burned out.

Perhaps you should give this marriage a decent burial. There'd be a fight over custody and access to your daughter, but your son would be a happier and more secure boy.

The alternative is to stick it out, enduring a life of increasing isolation and lack of love.

It isn't an alternative that I can recommend.

Revenge of a lost daughter

Dear Marje

After a very bitter divorce 22 years ago, my wife won custody of our small daughter and moved, making access to my child virtually impossible.

As the years went by, I sent her letters and presents, none of which were acknowledged. I know that my ex-wife, who is an evil woman, prevented the child from having any knowledge of me.

I married again and lost touch with my first wife. Then two years ago, out of the blue, my daughter turned up at our house.

My wife, who is kindness itself, offered her a home and I was absolutely delighted to have found her. But she is bent on destroying my marriage.

She is disruptive and abusive to my wife, manipulative and spiteful. She is out to make trouble and seems to be succeeding. My wife has now said either my daughter goes or she will. Can you, in your wisdom, advise me?

Says Marje

I do not think it requires very much wisdom to suggest to you that if you've got a modicum of it, you will send your daughter packing. She sounds awful, a chip off that old block, her evil mother.

Your ex-wife is, of course, the source of all your unhappiness and your daughter's unpleasant character.

She deliberately excluded you from having any influence or contact with your child and conditioned her from a very early age to hate you.

She almost undoubtedly grew up believing you'd abandoned her, and I think her main reason for wanting to track you down was to punish you for what, all her life, she was led to believe was your foul treatment of her and her mother.

She is a warped young woman, and although it's not easy to be charitable to someone like her, I guess she's more to be pitied than blamed.

It will be hard for you to turf her out. She's your own flesh and blood. You'll feel guilty when she slams your front door on her departure. You'll just have to cope with that, for though you have passed on genes to this young monster, you shouldn't consider yourself responsible for what she's turned out to be.

Your present wife now deserves a respite and some peace. Can you take her away for a nice holiday in the sun, perhaps, to recompense her for the dark days she's endured since she offered your daughter a home?

One of the sad aspects of all this is, what's to become of the girl? Someone so anti-social and bloody-minded isn't going to find it easy to make good relationships with anyone.

Still, that's no longer your problem. If a parent can ever manage to forget a child, perhaps you should do your best to try to forget yours.

Child quizzes mum on sofa sex session

Dear Marje

I am single mother with a six-and-a-half year old daughter. Three months ago I began an affair and life is now good. I think there could even be a future with him.

He and my daughter, whose father ditched me before she was born, get on really well. There's only one problem.

We have sex on the sofa in the living room of my small flat and though it's not very comfortable we manage.

But the other night my boyfriend did his back in and I always get a crick in the neck.

When we come to a climax we usually cry "ouch"!"

My boyfriend wants us to go into my bedroom to make love.

Also he says he'd like to stay over weekends, but I am worried about my daughter.

She is already very precocious, always asking how babies get in their mums' tummies and what do we actually do when she's in bed?

We'd be right next to her room if we went into mine.

Is she too young to be told the facts of life?

Says Marje

I have a feeling your daughter knows more about those facts than you imagine. That baby question is, I suspect, a cue for you to confirm what she already thinks.

It is impossible, in my view, to put an age limit on when children should be told.

The time to tell the facts is when they start asking the questions.

Your daughter sounds like she's six going on 16.

I bet she already knows the difference between boys and girls – at least physically. She will more than likely be part of a giggling group of kids exchanging playground information.

I think her curiosity is focused not on how the baby gets in the tummy, but what it is that you and your boyfriend do which makes you groan.

She probably lies awake listening intently for your climax.

You must now find the words to tell her. Be matter of fact.

Explain that when people are in love they kiss and cuddle and get excited and when the man's penis gets hard he puts in inside the woman between her legs and soon they reach what's called a climax.

That's when they cry out with pleasure and happiness, because this sex thing is a climax to love.

Tell her that a baby is sometimes the result of all this, though not always. That somewhat basic lesson should do for a start. You can then mention casually that what's-his-name might stay over next weekend and that he'll sleep in your bed.

If there are any further questions, answer them frankly.

There are books and leaflets, published by the Family Planning Association, which can help embarrassed tongue-tied parents deal with this tricky subject.

You are fortunate that your daughter asks you questions so that you can begin to prepare her for the adolescent problems she'll be facing all too soon.

Girl who hates her perfect brother

Dear Marje

My brother has ruined my life and I hate him. Now 30, he is four years old than me.

My parents idolised him. He was clever, handsome, good at games and a high achiever at school. He is now a successful accountant living with his glamorous girlfriend and yes, I am terribly jealous of him. To my parents I was a poor second best, very average at school, plain and mousey compared to his blond good looks. I became a secretary. Don't think I'm knocking it, I'm happy in my job.

My boyfriend, who I love, is a mere carpenter. My brother says with a sneer "how's your chippie, then, still busy with his chisel?"

He is a hateful patronising snob. The feeling of being a totally inadequate failure has haunted me all my life. My boyfriend said "write to Marje, she'll put you right." I only hope you can.

Says Marje

I hope your boyfriend's touching faith in me will be justified, but I am not the one to put you right. The only person who can sort out your tangled emotions is yourself.

You have a great ally in this sound and solid citizen you love and who, it's plain, loves you too. But although your brother sounds like an unpleasant jerk, I don't believe that he's to blame for your insecurity and very poor self-image.

He couldn't help being born with the advantage of good looks and academic distinction and athletic skills. But you can blame your parents for putting him on the pedestal he occupies.

Actually, you should feel sorry for him. He is forever lumbered with the self-image which was imposed on him from childhood.

I doubt if he's got many real friends as distinct from the hangers on most successful people acquire. The glamorous girlfriend is, perhaps, hardly more than just another symbol of his success.

Your parents damaged both of you. And I'm convinced the damage will prove to be more lasting in your brother's case. His lack of sensitivity and his patronising snobbery guarantee that he'll never earn real respect or deep love.

I hope I've managed to convince you that, far from feeling jealous of him, he's the one who ought to be jealous of you.

You have so much to be thankful for. Like your lovely chippie – whose profession is as skilled as any accountant's. It's immensely sad that parents like yours can't see the harm they do when they favour one child above the others.

But I am certain that with your boyfriend's love and support and your own hopefully revised view of yourself, you'll be able to lay the ghost of your miserable childhood forever.

Legacy of a drunken dad

Dear Marje

I vaguely remembered my father who left my mother when I was very young. On my 18th birthday two years ago, I had a very strong urge to see my father again. My mother died when I was 14 and I live with my stepfather.

Eventually I got hold of my father's address. I was advised to write to him and was given counselling. I contacted him and I was over the moon when he invited me to visit him.

Now I wish to God I'd never found him. He is shambling,

147

drink-sodden, foul-mouthed and disgusting and the only thing I'm thankful about is that he left my mother. She had some good years with my stepfather, who is a great guy and treats me like a son.

Now I feel very depressed. My father must have passed his genes on to me and I wish I could wipe him out of my life. Do you think it would help me to go back for some more counselling?

Says Marje

Yes, I'm sure it would, although even the most skilful and compassionate of counsellors wouldn't be able to help you to wipe your father from your mind and your life. And I'm sure no counsellor would attempt to.

I don't want to preempt any advice you might get, but I hope you'll be helped to come to terms with your parentage. As you rightly said, you've inherited some of his genes. But you had two parents, remember.

It's commonsense to assume that your father's genes must surely be balanced out by your mother's. There might even be a plus factor in your discovery of your unsavoury father. Now you know how not to live your life.

Follow his shambling, drunken footsteps, and you'd end up as disgusting as he is.

You were very lucky he abandoned you when you were too young to come under his influence. And very lucky indeed that your mother was able to rebuild her life with your good stepfather.

It's hard to know whether hereditary traits are a stronger influence than conditioning, but I'll stick my neck out and tell you I believe that growing up with a decent home life, a loving, happy mother and her equally loving husband has provided you with a legacy you can treasure.

I understand why people have such a desperate urge to find their roots and it's immensely disappointing, to put it mildly, when those roots turn out to be rotten. But surely the only thing that matters now is your self-image as it is at this moment.

You had a first-class role model in your stepfather, who stepped in to do the job which your natural father failed so dismally to do. In time, hopefully, your father will seem like a half-forgotten nightmare, one that may sometimes recur but as time goes by, will trouble you less and less.

Son is a mother's ruin

Dear Marje

I must sound quite horrible to you. My only son, aged 28, is married with a daughter. I like his wife very much and I love my grandchild but I can't stand my son.

He uses my flat for his own convenience. He leaves dirty clothes for me to wash, "borrows" cash which he never returns, makes long phone calls which he never pays for and expects me to cook meals at all hours for him.

He quarrels constantly with his wife and I get the feeling she's as fed up with him as I am. Sometimes he stays here three or four weeks, until they make it up again.

I am a pensioner with very little to live on. All I want now is peace in my old age.

I was 42 when he was born and perhaps because I was an older mother it's my fault he's like he is. What's more, he is a bully just like his father before him.

I don't know what advice, if any, you can give me but just telling someone helps a bit.

Says Marje

You do not seem to have had a lot of joy in your life, what with your bullying husband and this chip off the nasty old block, his son.

I realise why you've bottled up your feelings for so long. It's because you think it's unnatural for a mother to dislike her child.

I think that secretly, plenty of parents feel as you do at some point but I have always taken the view that love must be earned. You are worried that you might have influenced your son's present behaviour. Certainly, parental influence plays a big part in how children develop but your son had his father as an unfortunate role model.

He saw his dad bullying you and he assumes that if it was okay behaviour for his dad, it's okay for him. Especially as his

149

dad got away with it. The big question for you is, could you now, longing for that bit of peace, be strong enough to refuse to continue to put up with all this aggro?

Could you tell your son that from now on, food and lodgings at your flat is not on? That enough is enough and he must resolve his problems with his wife and let you enjoy the peace you yearn for?

If so, good for you and there'd be no need to feel guilty or bad about it. Perhaps if he could realise that by showing some respect and consideration for his mother, he'd even manage to earn your love.

Try to remember that while we can choose our friends, we can't choose our relatives. If we could, some of us would surely prefer not to have even known them.

And no, you are not horrible, just deeply disappointed to have a son you find so hard to love. But I'm glad you have a grandchild you do love and a nice daughter-in-law to give you comfort in what I hope will be a tranquil old age.

He can't resist a merry widow

Dear Marje

It's said that in the Spring a young man's fancy turns to thoughts of love. Perhaps it's the apple blossom or the leafy hedgerows, but my thoughts have definitely turned to love.

Except that I'm not a young man. I am 71. The object of my desire is a 46-year-old widow and her thoughts are on love, too.

We are planning to go away for a holiday, when I hope to consummate my passion. But my sister, two years my junior, says I am a disgusting, dirty old man.

I live in her house and she's made my life a misery since I told her about my girlfriend. She has refused to meet her. She has announced that if I go on that holiday, I will not be welcomed back.

I think she's jealous, she is certainly possessive. I don't want to end up living alone again but I do want to try my luck with the luscious widow. Advice, please, for an old boy who's lived like a monk since his wife passed on 12 years ago?

Says Marje

I'm not too sure it's love that has blossomed along with the darling buds of April. It sounds more like lust to me. As the sap rises in the apple trees it rises, too, in vigorous men and whether a man is 21 or 71 is neither here nor there.

But to confuse lust with love could be dodgy for a man in your situation, with your sister threatening you with eviction if you take off with your sweetheart.

If love it truly is, well you and I both know, from mature experience, that the world is, indeed, well lost for it. And if it's love, give your sister a brotherly smacker and tell her you'll find lodgings elsewhere. How is the widow fixed for a home? Any chance you could move in with her?

I note your proposed holiday is still at the planning stage and maybe it's as well to go slow for a few more weeks. You don't really need to go away to put your libido to the test. I realise you don't want to hang about until the sap has dried up and the Autumn leaves have fallen, but I'd hate you to lose your home and your sister's support for the sake of a gossamer dream that could melt in a spring shower. A modicum of patience and a further period of wooing would be wise.

There's another matter I must raise. You have been celibate for years, and as the great sexpert Dr Masters tells his patients who are knocking on a bit, use it or lose it. You've not been using it. It's to be hoped you've not lost it.

If it's love you both feel, quality performance doesn't matter much. But lust implies high expectations.

With the reservations I've outlined, I'd say that whether it's love or lust, give it a go before Winter finally sets in.

Incest slur mars dream romance

Dear Marje

My 25-year-old son has fallen in love with his first cousin, aged 23, and they are planning to get married. I am over the moon. She's smashing, and I know they will be happy.

They've both had other relationships but now they realise they are made for each other.

The fly in the ointment is her divorced mother, my sister. She can't accept it. She says it's incest, although her daughter has assured her mother the marriage will be perfectly legal.

Incidentally, she is right about that, isn't she? I'd like my sister to have confirmation from you. The young lovers are now having to put up with a lot of aggro from all the family. My sister is stupid, mischief-making and is causing no end of trouble. My only wish is for the happiness of my niece and my son. Can you please reassure them they stand as good a chance as any other couple in love?

Says Marje

They probably stand a better chance than most. They are young enough to be enthusiastic and old enough to make sensible judgements. And wise enough, from what I gather, to shrug off all the nonsense about incest and illegality.

I am delighted to confirm that marriage between first cousins is legal and the sex they'll enjoy is not incestuous.

Some people are concerned that the children of a first-cousin marriage might stand a slight risk of health problems.

It's not a bad idea for your son and future daughter-in-law to have a talk to a doctor, just in case there's a risk of a congenital problem. But it's a remote risk and I'd hate them to be alarmed.

It's sad though, isn't it, that sheer bloody ignorance, coupled by what seems like irrational prejudice, should get in the way of this young couple's happiness?

I can't help wondering if there's more to this than you think. Is your sister the sort of mother who'd think no man was ever going to be good enough for her daughter? Or, dare I express the nasty thought that she may be jealous of her daughter's happiness?

I do find it puzzling that your sister doesn't know she's talking a load of nonsense about incest and illegality. The subject has been well enough aired. That's what makes me suspicious. My blessings to your son and his girl and may they have a wonderful married life, despite her foolish mum. They're lucky that there's at least one sensible member of the family on their side.

Bitter daughter's revenge

Dear Marje

After my mother died, my father and I moved in with my grandparents. But my dad was lonely and I was really pleased when he started dating a neighbour. He's going to marry her soon.

I thought she'd be like a second mother to me. My gran is great but she's too old to understand someone my age, which is 16, and I really did want to get close to this woman. But she is a cunning liar. She pretended she cared about me, but I soon realised it was sheer window-dressing.

Once she'd got my dad, she showed me her true colours. There was a lot of bitterness and my father blamed me, of course. She can do no wrong.

They expect me to live with them, but I won't and I won't go to the wedding either. My father has got no loyalty to me, only to this bogus woman. I'll stay with my grandparents. But my gran wants me to apologise to my dad and go to this wedding. I suppose I'll have to go so as not to upset her, but can you understand my feelings?

Says Marje

Yes. I can understand them quite well. It's tough for a 16-year-old girl to be going through all the emotional problems of adolescence without a mother's shoulder to cry on.

I understand, too, your disappointment when your father's fiancee didn't measure up to your image of a mother-substitute, but it was an unreal image.

You didn't or couldn't know her well enough to be her instant daughter. A relationship like that has to grow and love has to be earned by both parties. Clearly you got up each other's noses before you had a chance to establish any affectionate ties. I bet she wanted you for a substitute daughter as much as you wanted her mother-love and I don't know, on account of you've not told me the whole story, which one started the aggro first. I do know, though, that your dad must be a very unhappy man, despite his good fortune in meeting someone he loves and who loves him. For you have alienated yourself by being hateful to his wife-to-be.

Maybe she is cunning and bogus, whatever you mean by that, but he loves her and wouldn't it be great for him if you could be a bit bogus yourself and pretend you're happy he's marrying her?

You are making a big drama out of his disloyalty to you because he loves her, but he can love her and still love you and I'm sure he does, even though you're being a right pain.

Your gran might not live in your hip teenage world, but she's right on when she tells you to apologise to your pa.

And go out tomorrow and buy a wedding present, even if you have to cadge the cash for it from your father.

RELATIONSHIPS

She longs for more passion

Dear Marje

My first husband was a womanising Jack the Lad – but life was one long laugh. We went to clubs and pubs, drank a lot, did some drugs, had a ball.

But after five years, I found out he was having a ball with other women, too, and I divorced him.

Then I met a man who was the opposite of my husband. We have just celebrated – with mineral water – our first anniversary. And I can't believe what a fool I've been. It's a near-sexless marriage, with no passion and no satisfaction for me, though he seems satisfied enough.

He doesn't want to go out, is happy to watch the box for hours. And I am sick to death of him. At 44, I'm set for a life of total frustration. Or am I? Wouldn't you agree I'd be wise to leave him now while I'm young enough to find someone else?

Says Marje

Yes, I would – but as much for your husband's sake as for yours. I can't imagine what he's done to deserve such a fate. It's easy to see why you grabbed him.

He had all the qualities your first husband lacked.

I think at 44, you are immature and you needn't rage at me for saying so. It will help you to face facts, difficult as they may be to stomach.

Your overview of your first marriage was like a teenager's vision of bliss. Boozing, clubbing, pub crawling, drugging and uninhibited sex. Nothing wrong with that last element. It was probably the least harmful aspect of your marriage.

When you wed your Jack you wanted to enjoy the lifestyle of a 15-year-old and it seems to me you've hardly aged since. You couldn't see, could you, that your present husband was never going to match up to the first one? But would you want all that senseless racketing again? At 44? I can understand why you're so frustrated in bed with this unromantic man, but I advise you to see this as a challenge.

You've a student on your hands. You know more about sexual techniques than he's probably ever heard of. He might enjoy more exciting ways of spending those quiet evenings at home than you imagine. You could suggest sexy videos perhaps, rather than BBC2, and raise his expectations and your hopes.

But if by now you are too disenchanted even to try, then yes, release him and yourself. But think very hard about the lonely life of an unloved divorcee. You may not get a third chance.

Lies of a cruel conman

Dear Marje

I had just broken up with my married lover. I thought I'd never get over it and was feeling very low when I met another man at work.

The new man restored my self-confidence. He told me he was divorced and lived with his sister who looked after his two small daughters.

We talked about getting engaged. We had sex as often as we could, though he explained he had to spend his evenings with his motherless children and I didn't for a moment resent it.

Then one day he failed to turn up at the office and I was worried in case he was ill and I got his address from his secretary and went to his house.

I assumed the women who opened the door was his sister. She wasn't. She was his wife.

How could a man apparently so decent be such a cruel liar? How could he swear he loved me?

How could I have been so easily conned? And how am I ever going to get over this second terrible blow?

Says Marje

Let's look first at the questions you ask. All too many apparently decent men are cruel liars. Bloody cruel liars. Your

156

second love realised he'd have to lie to get you under the duvet or in the back seat of the car or wherever you did your heavy breathing.

If he'd announced at the first tender touching of hands that he had a wife and a couple of children, he wouldn't have stood much chance with a woman so obviously looking for security.

How could he swear he loved you? Easy. The words come naturally to men like him. Only the ones who hesitate before committing themselves are as decent as you thought he was.

As for how you could so easily have been conned, well you were waiting to be.

A rejected woman is highly vulnerable. By your own admission, he restored your self respect and he made you feel good and loved and wanted and you were easily lured into the bed or the car's back seat.

This man has left you in an even worse condition than you were before. Much worse, for you had to face the humiliation of confronting his wife.

If there's a grain of comfort anywhere for you, you can bet he got the handbagging of his life from her. I should think he'll be absent from work for several days.

The final question you posed was how are you ever going to get over this awful blow? The way you got over the first one, I guess.

But I won't pretend it'll be easy. There will be an immense temptation to grab the first man you meet to restore your ego.

Here's hoping that the third time will be lucky for you. Incidentally, I don't offer his secretary much hope of job security, though you should be grateful to her.

If she hadn't been such a blabbermouth, you'd still be living in that Fool's Paradise, believing those lies and loving a totally worthless man.

Despair of a spurned lover

Dear Marje

Mine was a marriage in name only, when five years ago I met the woman I love.

I assured her that when my youngest child reached 16, I would divorce my wife so we could marry. She said she

loved me so much she'd wait forever. My wife knew there
was someone else. But for everyone's sake, my girlfriend
and I were discreet. I saw her regularly at her house, we
spent marvellous holidays together and at 47, I looked
forward to spending the rest of my life with her.

Last week she told me it was all over. She says there's no
one else. She's simply, in her words, "gone off the boil".

Not only am I heartbroken but I am baffled by what has
happened.

My marriage has ended, my teenage children have little
time for their father and I've lost my partner.

Can you explain how a woman who professed to love a
man as she did can behave with such cruelty?

Says Marje

When you say the woman you love has behaved cruelly, are
you implying, perhaps, that she is out to punish you?

And if so, why? You seem to have done all the right things.
You didn't pack in your marriage or shirk your
responsibilities. You were conscientious as a husband and a
lover.

And you didn't promise this woman you'd marry her as soon
as a divorce became practicable and then, as men sometimes
do, go back on that promise.

No wonder you ask yourself why she has given you the
elbow.

I think it's because she has simply stopped loving you. The
magic has gone. But I don't think it's a sudden feeling of
disenchantment. I don't believe she woke up one morning and
decided she'd had it.

It's much more likely that she'd begun to have doubts some
time ago and the catalyst was your announcement that the
divorce was going through.

It probably suited her to have a part-time lover with whom to
share a few pleasant hours and holidays.

Rather nice for her, actually. She had the companionship and
the sex and she didn't have to wash your boxer shorts and
socks, cook your meals, watch telly programmes of your
choice and deal with your wrath when the housekeeping
budget bust yet again. She was able to enjoy all the
advantages of part-time non-marriage, with none of the

disadvantages of being wife, mother and domestic drudge. And when marriage became a real possibility, she realised she didn't love you enough to take all that on board.

True, her sudden announcement was a cruel shock and I feel very sorry for you.

But I'd feel even more sorry if she married you out of a sense of duty and ditched you six months later, as it's possible she would.

She liked being a mistress. She simply didn't want to be a wife. And a good many wives wouldn't blame her.

Real hell of a marriage

Dear Marje

I absolutely detest my wife and there's no doubt she hates me too. She is the most aggressive, sour, cold person I have ever known. She is also foul-mouthed and slovenly.

Sometimes, I wonder how I was ever mad enough to marry her. I only did it because I got her pregnant when she was 17, though I promise you she led me on.

I am nine years older than her. She never stops nagging and complaining about being short of money though she spends plenty on drink and cigarettes.

After 10 years of this hell, we both decided to go for counselling but it didn't work. The only good to have come out of it all is my wonderful kids. They're the reason I've stayed. But they realise what's going on.

Should I stay for their sake or would it be better for them if I left?

Says Marje

They don't stand much chance of growing up in a tranquil, loving home anyway, do they, poor little devils?

This is one of those judgment of Solomon issues I dread, for nothing I can suggest will solve this problem.

Perhaps if you separated and applied to the court for custody of the children, you might get it but they'd be deprived of a mother they presumably love.

Could you, given you got lucky, look after them? One thing

159

bothers me. I know why you hate your wife. But why does she hate you? Are you a blameless angel in all this?

I don't like one bit the description of your "courtship" and the reason why you got married. A 17-year-old trapping a man of 26 by deliberately getting herself pregnant? That's a tall one.

Condoms weren't invented last week. Didn't you carry a couple in your pocket? And if not, why not? You put all the blame for everything on her. That's why I am so suspicious. She sounds horrendous, I agree. But you are so biased and uncompromising that I can't help feeling this a case of pots calling kettles black.

Maybe one hope would be to go back for more counselling but determined this time to stick it out and work at it.

Both of you. I don't see how either of you can go on living together in such mutual and destructive hatred.

I have somewhat dodged your question. I'm scared of giving you a bum steer. Scared, not for you, but for your children.

But ultimately I feel that if you can't, for their sake, try to work something out together then yes, in the end they might be better off without having to witness their parents' daily fights. It's unlikely there will be any winners in this sad family saga.

Disgusted by his dirty dancing

Dear Marje

After my divorce, I was lucky enough to meet a dreamy man. He was great in bed and great to look at and I was over the moon when he said: "Let's get married."

We did just that a year ago but it has been a year of torment for me. He made no secret that he'd had plenty of women before me but he said all that was behind him when he met me.

Women were crazy about him and I didn't blame them. I was happy because I was the one who got him. But the way he goes on, no one would believe he was married.

He flirts. He touches women up and makes suggestive remarks in front of me.

I now refuse to go to discos because of the sexy way he dances with girls. He almost does it with them in public! I'm still crazy about him but I can't be doing with all this.

My mum says she knew all along what he was like and she says I should leave him now before he breaks my heart. Do you agree with her?

Says Marje

I can see why your mum is worried about you and your marriage to this sexy Jack the Lad. She doesn't think you'll be enjoying your twilight Darby and Joan days together and I'm inclined to go along with her opinion.

But unlike her, I reckon you should give this marriage a chance.

It's only been a year since you plighted your troth with Jacko. I think that despite all his past experiences with other females he is still hardly more than a boy whatever age he is now.

In fact, he's the type who could continue to be immature even after he picks up his bus pass. There are plenty of men who need to be constantly reassured that they are desirable to women, even though they love their wives passionately.

Your husband was endearingly honest. He told you about his past exploits so, like your mother, you knew what he was like. But unlike your mother, you loved him and still do, despite his antics.

I don't suppose he's got the slightest idea how much he humiliates you. He's too insensitive to realise that. You might mention it to him but he'll probably be amazed that he hurts you.

I'm not sure if you're wise to ban the disco sessions. The danger of this kind of ban is that if he really did seriously want to have sex with someone else, he'd do it behind your back.

I think that while he's fooling around in your presence, it's nothing more than schoolboy nonsense. It would be very sad if you felt you should take your mum's advice. But give it a little longer. That daft-as-a-brush kid you married needs a stable home-life with a woman who loves him.

As he gets older, he'll be a laughing stock among the girls who he touches up. Then he'll discover how soul-destroying humiliation can be.

Work-out for a fit marriage

Dear Marje

I am very friendly with a girl I met at my Keep-Fit class. She has a great sense of humour and makes all the boring working-out fun.

Then one night I asked her to pop in to meet my husband. She soon had him eating out of her hand, flattering him and telling him she could see why he didn't need to go to Keep-Fit.

Within half an hour he was fixing up a foursome evening out. The evening was a disaster for me. She is a very manipulative person. She got the men hanging on her every word and the come-on looks made me feel sick.

Now things between me and my husband are tense and the other evening he actually asked me why I'm not more like her.

I don't know what to do. Perhaps I should pack in the Keep-Fit and stop seeing her, except that the damage is done now and I can't see how it can be undone, unless you've got any ideas?

Says Marje

You go to Keep-Fit class to lose a few inches off your hips but you are also in danger of losing much more, like a sense of proportion. As well as your easily-manipulated husband.

Why don't you pick up a few tricks from your friend? From the sound of it she knows them all. She is well aware that the way to a man's heart is through flattery and you've observed at first hand how effective it is.

Have you ever told your husband he's in such perfect shape Keep-Fit is the last thing he needs? Do you hang on his every word and nod eagerly when he expresses an opinion? Or is your mind elsewhere, counting calories perhaps?

It would be interesting to know why you go every week to sweat off a few pounds. Some people join these groups simply because it's one way to broaden their social lives at the same time as narrowing their waistlines.

Others of course, have a genuine desire to look leaner and feel fitter, either to improve their self-image or because they feel they have to compete with the maddeningly-thin friends who could eat two boxes of chocolates a day without gaining an ounce.

Others – and perhaps you are in this group – fear that if they let themselves get too podgy, they'll lose the love of a good man. You feel very insecure about your marriage but here you have a wonderful opportunity to learn from an expert that, while a few inches more or less around the hips are irrelevant, flattery will get you everywhere.

I suggest you carry on with the Keep-Fit but be sparing with your invitations. And remember you can learn more useful lessons from this knowing girl than you'll ever get from the teacher in your class.

He's lost that loving feeling

Dear Marje

I have just "celebrated" my seventh wedding anniversary by lying awake all night alone. He's never forgotten one before.

Don't get me wrong. I am quite used to sleeping alone.

I knew what it would be like when I married a long-distance truck driver. But until the past few months, I never felt lonely or neglected like I do now. He was once a really loving man. He rang me every night without fail, wherever he was.

He'd send me flowers for no particular reason and write little notes saying: "Loving you, missing you." When I expected him home, I always made myself look great for him, wearing the see-through undies he likes and we had really fantastic sex.

Now, when he comes home he's off-hand and surly and the love notes and the flowers have stopped coming. I get a brief phone call once a week if I'm lucky.

I can't believe he's got another woman. He'd hardly have time. But what am I to believe, and what can I do to sort all this out?

Says Marje

We don't hear so much these days about the seven-year itch, partly perhaps because nowadays the itching can begin within seven days, so dramatically have standards of fidelity faltered.

But there could be a much less sinister explanation for your husband's apparent neglect. Long-distance drivers, like countless other citizens, are worried sick about their jobs and their families' security.

Your silly trucker wouldn't realise, as he stares through his windscreen these dark mornings, that his romantic wife can't understand why he's less romantic than he used to be.

I think he simply takes it for granted that you'll be there in your see-throughs when he climbs wearily out of his cab and heads for home.

If he's a bit surly, it's probably because he's worried. The thought of scribbling tender little love notes simply doesn't enter his anxious head.

If every marriage ended because an absent-minded husband forgot an anniversary, there'd be hardly any marriages left. Next time he comes home, why not ask him if he's got something bothering him, and if so, how can you help?

Be careful not to whine or moan and don't, repeat don't, have a go at him about the forgotten anniversary. Give over feeling so sorry for yourself and try to feel sorry for him, doing a rough old job and worrying in case he loses it.

I remember a long-distance trucker once telling me it's one of the loneliest jobs in the world. I can believe it and so should you. My guess is that he's simply trying to protect you from anxiety. Mop up your tears – and try to protect him from his.

Second thoughts over her lost stud

Dear Marje

I had longed for a baby even before I started living with my boyfriend and I was in heaven when I got pregnant.

But after my son was born, the relationship deteriorated.

All I cared about was the baby. I became indifferent to his father and our sex life was non-existent.

Then, during a quarrel, I told him that I'd only ever wanted him to father my child, that I'd never loved him and he could clear out.

I was stupid enough to believe that I could provide my son with everything he needed. It didn't occur to me that the baby's father might want him, too.

For the past two years he has come to see him every weekend, and the child and his father idolise each other.

I realise, now it's too late, that I've let a very special man go and I'd do anything to get him back.

Please print this as a warning to other girls who might be as foolish as I've been.

Says Marje

It's charitable of you to be so concerned about the fate of other girls, but very few people heed warnings like yours or learn lessons from other people's disasters.

They figure that such disasters can only happen to others, not to them.

The one hopeful aspect of your sad letter was your recognition of the pain your behaviour has brought to the three main characters in this drama.

No need for me to remind you and other foolish girls that treating a man merely as a stud to fulfil a maternal longing will scare even the wimpiest of them away.

I see little chance of your baby's father forgiving easily the major insult to his manhood you inflicted on him.

But the one glimmer of hope is that you see him regularly, and there's the tiniest spark between you still, in time, it might be re-ignited.

Perhaps you could tentatively suggest to him that family outings with the little boy would be good for him and would help him to grow up knowing that both his parents are united in their longing for his well-being.

Suggest trips for the three of you to the zoo or a theme park or just to roam around together as a family.

And while you are slowly building up these family ties, you and the man you shed may, perhaps, be re-building your relationship. There are no swift cures that I can offer you. You will have to think up ways to convince him he's important to you as well as to the child.

Be patient. There's plenty of time. Only if and when he feels he can trust you will he feel secure enough to consider making that family threesome permanent.

Try to make an opportunity to tell him how remorseful and regretful you are about the shabby way you treated him. I hope for your sake and your son's he'll listen and respond.

He sounds like a nice, loving bloke. Show him that you appreciate him now, even though you were too stupid to in the past. And if only one foolish girl is warned by your mistake, I'm very glad indeed to have printed your letter.

SEX DIFFICULTIES

Love in the dark for shy wife

Dear Marje

My wife, who is 47, has just told been told she must have a hysterectomy and she is very worried and depressed.

She seems to think it means the end of normal life.

She has always been shy and absurdly modest. She won't make love with the light on or in the nude. In fact she's not very keen on it in her pyjamas in the dark. I'll admit I've had several other more exciting women during our 20 years of marriage.

I was amazed when she asked me if I thought there'd be no more love-making after the operation and I'm not sure if she hopes there won't be or if she's concerned in case there isn't.

You may wonder why I don't just ask her. In a marriage like ours, sex has simply never been discussed – only performed in near-silence.

Should I talk to her doctor, do you think, or try to persuade her to?

Says Marje

Certainly the time has come for some earnest discussion in your marriage. You both seem to have been silent for far too long and it won't be easy for either of you to loosen your tongues – and your minds.

But your wife has made a nervous, tentative start. It's a bonus that she's actually been able to express her concern, to let you know she's scared and depressed.

Almost every woman facing a hysterectomy shares similar worries. Fearsome thoughts disturb their nights. "Will I emerge from the anaesthetic a sexless creature, unable ever again to respond to a man? Will I age overnight"?

These are the two main fears. A doctor with a spare couple of minutes should reassure his patient with a firm NO in reply to these questions. Most doctors do, if they're asked. Some thoughtful ones don't even wait to be asked.

From your description of your pathetic wife's attitude to life and love, I'd say that secretly, she's hoping the operation will release her from the burden of sex. That tiny signal she's offered which suggests a willingness – even perhaps, a hope of talking about her fears – could be a frail lifeline to your unsatisfactory marriage.

I suggest you explain that you've had a word with someone who seems to know about the op and you've been told that, after a few weeks of convalescence and rest, unless there are complications, she'll be as good as new.

Better, in fact, because she'll be in cracking good health again. But reassure her that you'll put no pressure on her to pull down her pyjama bottoms – you'll just be there if she feels like a comforting cuddle.

I know it's tough to face the possibility that you'll always have to find fulfilling sex outside your marriage.

But you don't indicate that you have ever thought of leaving your wife and I hope you won't, even though it's such an arid relationship.

She can't confess she's faking it

Dear Marje

You often give advice to men who suffer problems such as premature ejaculation or impotence, but you seldom mention women who find it difficult to reach orgasm.

Is this because fewer women write about this or is it because women are reluctant or too embarrassed to seek help?

My husband got help when he wrote to you and things are greatly improved. Now I need help. I very rarely reach a climax and in our 14 years of marriage I have faked orgasms to please my husband.

I am a shy, introverted person – frigid perhaps – and find it difficult to talk about sex. Some of my women friends don't hesitate and I long to tell them my problem but I can't. It's taken me ages to pluck up courage to write to you and I hope you can help me.

168

Says Marje

I am pretty sure just as many women as men have sexual difficulties. But more men, I think, panic. Any sign of weakness or disorder "down there" and a man fears his masculinity is threatened.

Women, though, don't reckon they are not womanly if they fail to reach orgasm.

Your problem, I assure you, is not insoluble. It doesn't mean you are frigid because you can't reach a climax.

But your shyness and introverted nature do mean you may be scared of losing control. Any difficulties in your marriage could add to the problem. But if you love your husband and he loves you, stop worrying and start taking positive action.

You don't tell me if your husband is a patient lover. Perhaps he would pay more attention to your needs, if only you could tell him what they are.

Maybe now that you've spelled them out to me, you will be able to whisper a few instructions to him. Or guide his hand, but not his now-lively penis, not yet. There's a way to go before you get to that stage.,

I shall send you my orgasm leaflet which you should read with your husband. He'd have needed your help as you'll need his. And in the end, both of you will benefit by greatly enhanced sexual fulfillment.

And one day I bet you'll be joining in those all-girl discussions and boasting along with the best of them. Good luck and I am glad you wrote.

When love means saying sorry

Dear Marje

The word I'm beginning to hate most is "sorry". Night after night, and sometimes in the morning, my husband mutters that word as, yet again, what he starts out to do ends a few seconds later.

Premature ejaculation is spoiling our marriage. But I am not bothered about it for myself, only for him.

Of course, it would be wonderful if we were able to enjoy

169

long stretches of foreplay before he entered me and ejaculated. But he can't wait.

I love him – and as long as he loves me too, that's all I care about. I know he does, and this is why he's so distressed and forever apologising. He knows how to satisfy me, but feels he's a failure and it's affecting him in all sorts of ways. He is more and more withdrawn, not from me, but from our friends. He used to be sociable – now he's moody.

How can I help him? He is 52 and he was married before, but there was no problem with his first wife, so could I in some way be responsible?

Says Marje

I can't imagine how you could possibly be responsible in any way for your husband's problem.

You sound like a perfect wife caring far more about his happiness than your own.

I have no way of knowing why he has no control over his ejaculation, but I can tell you – and I hope you'll tell him – that premature ejaculation is probably the most common of all male sexual problems.

It happens in good marriages like yours, or in quarrelsome ones, and it's almost always psychological. But as your husband had no problems in the past, it would be a good idea to get a doctor to give him a check-up.

All the doctors I've talked to tell me physical causes are very rare, and almost always the problem is in the mind. One of your husband's difficulties could be over-anxiety to satisfy you.

If he didn't much care whether his first wife was satisfied or not, he was probably intent more on his own gratification than on hers.

Guilt is another possible reason for the problem.

A nice man like your husband would have felt to some extent responsible for the marriage break-up, even if his first wife was a bad-tempered bitch who'd slept with 50 other men. Now for the good news. Provided a couple work together, the problem can be controlled. Nearly all men who suffer from premature ejaculation are likely to make a full recovery using what's known as the "stop-start" method. This requires the co-

170

operation of the man's partner and considerable patience from both parties. The method is clearly explained in a leaflet I've written.

There is step-by-step guidance, and if you'd write and let me have an address where I can post it, I'll send it to you – or to anybody else who'd like one.

I hope very much it will help you to wipe that hated word "sorry" from your husband's bedtime vocabulary.

It would be wonderful if instead he could murmur: "Was it as good for you as it was for me? Great, let's do it again."

Her ideal husband has a small problem

Dear Marje

This is a very difficult letter for me to write. I am almost too embarrassed to tell you what my problem is but I really do need help. Or rather, my husband does. He is not very well endowed down there, he's quite small in fact. We have been married two years and he seems to be okay when we make love but every time we do he asks me if he satisfies me.

He is anxious about his performance and constantly seeks reassurance.

He has always been rather shy. He says at school the other boys ribbed him unmercifully. Yet he's tall and well-built.

I have no experience of other men and I don't know whether he's got anything to worry about.

I keep telling him size doesn't matter, all I care about is that we love one another but I know he gets depressed. How can I convince him that he's not the freak he seems to think he is?

Says Marje

You are obviously a loving and concerned wife but you are

making the biggest mistake of your life in telling your husband the size of his penis doesn't matter.

It matters like hell to him. I know you are trying to reassure him but you are going the wrong way about it. The size of his penis is as important to a man as the size of her breasts are to a woman.

If yours were as flat as a plate, would you feel great if your loved one said he really appreciates your plate-like non-boobs?

Of course not. You'd feel terrible and you couldn't bear him even to look at them, let alone caress them. Your husband probably wears pyjamas in bed rather than reveal his poor little willy to you. If he raises the subject of his size again, simply tell him he's perfect.

A perfect lover and a perfect husband and you love him to death. You could, if he insists on pushing the subject, tell him you read somewhere (you are reading it here) that size is quite irrelevant to performance.

Some well-hung gents are poor lovers, often more concerned with their own glorious image than with satisfying their partners.

You could also mention you read that a woman's vagina is constructed to accommodate practically any size, from mini to maxi. You must tell him every time he makes love to you, how wonderful it was and you know it was as good for him as it was for you.

Hopefully, with positive thinking and talking, his post-coital depression will lift.

He needs constant but subtle reassurance that he can be proud of his manhood. Knowing that you're proud of it will hopefully convince him that he can be as well.

Sex that always ends in tears

Dear Marje

My wife and I have only been married for four months and I'm already worried about a problem. When we make love she nearly always cries.

I am sure I don't hurt her during sex. She used to cry when we did it before we got married, but I thought then it was only because she might be feeling insecure.

I've asked her if I cause her pain or if I've done anything to upset her, but she says she doesn't know why she cries. She says that when she gets to a certain point in our lovemaking, she can't contain her feelings.

I've tried to be gentle with her. Neither of us had much experience with other partners but we love each other and we're happy in every other way. I feel very lucky to have found her. But this crying is causing us both a lot of worry. Can you help by telling us what you think is wrong with her?

Says Marje

Tonight when you and your wife get into bed and fall on each other panting with desire, set about enjoying a prolonged bout of lovemaking. And when your wife finally reaches her orgasm and begins to sob, congratulate yourself.

Those cries are simply her reaction to orgasm. Some women grunt, moan or simply murmur breathlessly "more, more".

But many like your wife, weep at the moment of truth and that's the moment when you should gently cradle her head against your shoulder, while you tell her how much you love her and ask her if it was as good for her as it was for you.

Her reaction is a common one. But there's one point I should make. She's probably a highly emotional girl and with girls like this the tears flow because the charged moments prior to orgasm are mixed with hidden feelings of guilt or even shame, that the climax to love is so blissful.

A lot of women are brought up to believe it's not very nice to be seen and heard enjoying it.

This might seem far-fetched to you, but I assure you that even if a touch of guilt or shame is behind the weeping, the main reason for the tears is the release of the tension that foreplay arouses.

Incidentally, excuse me for mentioning it, but since you wrote in blunt terms I must be equally blunt. Are you giving her enough? Foreplay, I mean.

Women are usually slower to climax than men. A lusty man in a hurry can deprive his partner of the stimulation she needs.

Also, again if you'll excuse me, many lucky women can have several orgasms – a series of them – to one male emission but not a lot of men realise this. Maybe one reason for your wife's tears is that she wants bit more loving than she's getting, but isn't bold enough to mention it.

There, then, I've been bold on her behalf. Have a wonderful night tonight.

Why he switches off

Dear Marje

My husband, who is 61, recently had a prostate operation. He has never wanted to talk about sex, though he's eager enough to have it. His vigorous appetite hasn't diminished over the 30 years of our marriage.

I'm as keen as he is and the success of our sex life has contributed to our happy marriage. But since the operation he has simply switched off.

He lies with his back to me in bed and when I try to discuss it, he clams up. Women friends whose husbands have had this job done tell me they don't have this problem. I am sure you will suggest my husband discusses it with his doctor. But you don't know my husband, or his doctor. My husband won't listen to advice and the doctor is sour and unhelpful.

Can you give me any comfort for the future or must I accept that this aspect of my life is over?

Says Marje

Certainly you mustn't accept for a moment that from now on you need lead a sexless life. Many men of your husband's generation find it very difficult indeed to refer to any problem "down there".

Their private parts are just that: Private. Even where their nearest and dearest is concerned. You sound like a lively, uninhibited lady who enjoys raunchy conversations with women friends, and it must be extremely frustrating for you to have to cope with your uptight man.

When all his parts were in good working order, clearly there was no need for earnest discussion. But men get very worried indeed if they fear there's a threat to their manhood and it's bad luck he has such an unhelpful doctor. A few kind words from him would swiftly reassure you both.

I, too, have friends whose spouses have had this job done. I was talking to one just the other day. She said that only a few weeks after he came out of hospital he was at it again and almost as good as new. And he's no chicken, either.

It appears that there is a minor change in the way the affected member performs. But it was indeed performing and soon stimulated into action with a little encouragement from her.

I hope my friend's experience reassures you. It should, for her husband's recovery from this comparatively simple surgical routine is commonplace.

Sometimes something goes amiss but usually it can be rectified quite easily. I think your best plan would be to thrust this page at your husband with a request to read it.

Give him a bit more time to recover his health and strength then use every trick in your book to restore his confidence and his libido.

I'm sure you've plenty up your sleeve. I guarantee it won't be long before he once again rolls over towards you in bed instead of foolishly turning his back.

Guilt spoils sex with a new wife

Dear Marje

At the young age of 28, I became a widower after a tragic accident ended my wife's life. We had been married only four years.

She was five months' pregnant when I lost her – and lost all hope of ever being happy again. Then, three years after the accident, I met a lovely woman who has done everything possible to help me to recover.

Because of her, I was able to come to terms with my loss, and we married 10 months ago. I suppose nothing can ever match up to first love, but I do love my wife deeply. Sadly, though, I cannot love her passionately. We have sex and I do know I satisfy her. I have no physical sexual problem. I get strong erections and she is responsive and exciting in bed. But everything is spoiled for me by the enormous

175

sense of guilt I suffer afterwards.

She sleeps contentedly beside me while I lie awake in misery because, ludicrous as it may sound, I feel I am being unfaithful to my first wife. Have you ever come across this problem before?

Says Marje

Yes, I have, many times. It's not an uncommon problem. You are more fortunate than some men, whose guilt makes them impotent and whose second marriages often fail because resentful second wives can't understand why a man is still unable to wipe out the memory of a first wife when he falls in love again.

You are fortunate, too, in your second wife. I have to argue with you when you say that nothing can ever match up to first love. That simply isn't true. Your first love perished while that love was still unspoilt, but only rarely are happy marriages sustained at that level of bliss.

As time goes by, tensions are pretty inevitable and although it's wonderful that you still cherish such loving memories, the reality would almost certainly have become more mundane. No one's perfect, but in your mind your first wife was and her death left your notion of love and marriage in an unreal time warp.

You say you feel guilty and unfaithful to your first wife when you make love to your second.

But has it ever occurred to you that if she'd lived, you in restless middle-age might well have occasionally been an unfaithful husband?

Don't be shocked when I say this. I'm only being realistic. Countless happily married men have casual affairs and I often wonder how many of them are overwhelmed by guilt.

Not too many I suspect, unless their wives find out.

I can't offer you any magic solutions. I can only remind you that because your first young wife loved you as deeply as you loved her, she'd want you to be happy and contented now with the mature woman who has done so much to help you to cope with your sorrow.

I hope your new wife's reward will be your guilt-free love. She deserves it and so do you.

He's lost his loving urge

Dear Marje

Six years ago I had a miscarriage, and my husband hasn't made love to me since.

I've tried everything to turn him on – sexy underwear, suggesting erotic experiments, flirting with him – but he doesn't react.

He likes to fondle me and that's all. And after years of trying I feel like giving up. But we're both only 38 and I'm very frustrated.

It's obvious he must be too, because a few weeks ago I discovered him masturbating over a porn magazine and I went through the roof.

I asked him why, if he could do this, he couldn't make love to me and he said he didn't know. When I threatened him with divorce, he begged me not to leave him.

We are quarrelling all the time and it's getting me down and I'm sure it's affecting my health. What can I do to get my husband to have a normal loving relationship with me?

Says Marje

Pity your husband didn't write to me instead of you. He might have been able to explain to an objective stranger why he can no longer fulfill his sexual needs with you, rather than seek release with a dirty mag on his lap.

I can only make wild guesses and I could be wildly wrong. Perhaps he feels that he was in some way responsible for your miscarriage.

Some men find it difficult to have sex after a baby's birth.

One man described it to me as a "shuddering distaste". Another said he found pregnancy offputting.

Luckily for the majority of couples, pregnancy and childbirth are the ultimate expression of love.

I can only guess that your husband is consumed with guilt about the loss of your baby to the extent that he simply can't rationalise it. Perhaps you'll find it too difficult to do what I suggest. Which is, calm down and set up a cosy cuddling session. Whisper that you understand the mag incident, you're sorry you blew your top and will he please let you do to him what he was doing with that magazine.

In plain words, masturbate him. He'll appreciate it and enjoy it and if you repeat it frequently, he will, I think, gradually become less inhibited towards you.

He will relate sexual gratification to you. You might now be thinking: "Whoa, what's in all this for me? How do I get my gratification?" You can practise DIY for the time being.

Sexual therapy would help your husband – your GP could organise it – but if you can be his own personal private therapist, I believe it will bring you closer to each other in every possible way.

Married 22 years and still a virgin

Dear Marje

I've just put down the phone after a conversation with the doctor's receptionist, who was trying to make an appointment for me to have a smear test. I've had three calls from the doctor but I want to avoid the test because after 22 years of marriage, I am still a virgin.

My husband and I have never managed to make love. And strange though it may sound in this sex-obsessed age, we've never missed it. We're happily married and we give each other satisfaction. I don't want to become some kind of curiosity, examined by medical students and giggled at by nurses. I have my pride and I'm not ill. How can I tell them to leave me alone?

Says Marje

Three rousing, hearty cheers from me for your doctor. He or she deserves a much more positive response to his medical care and sense of responsibility than he's had from you.

He won't give a damn whether or not you're a virgin. All he's interested in is protecting your health. You don't mention your age, but it's clear you've reached the time in your life when it's sensible to make sure nothing is threatening it. When I say nothing, I mean cancer.

Smear-testing has saved the lives of countless vulnerable

women.

I sympathise with your reluctance to reveal to the doctor that sex has never been on the agenda of your married life.

It's not clear whether the problem is yours or your husband's. Maybe you suffer from what's called vaginismus – the name for a too-tight vagina.

You can forget all those fears about giggling nurses and prurient medical students. Believe me, your vagina will be no novelty for them. They've seen them in all shapes and sizes and conditions.

What makes me sad is that vaginismus can be cured very easily and if your husband has some genital problem, the chances are that it too, can be sorted out without much difficulty.

All these years, the pair of you have been making do with a substitute for perfect sex when perfection is achievable. And how much more wonderful it would be to enjoy the real thing.

Your smear test could, in fact, be a great blessing, apart from its usual purpose. It will give you the opportunity to tell your good doctor the truth. Forget your daft, totally unnecessary pride and ring up now for that appointment.

POWER STRUGGLES

Battling for love

Dear Marje

My girlfriend and I have lived together for three years. On the whole we're happy, until she deliberately picks a quarrel and storms off home to her mother's.

I'm easy-going and I hate these fights and can't understand why she starts them. Sometimes she stays away for days, sometimes it's weeks.

She comes back loving but not the least bit remorseful. I've offered to marry her but the last time I mentioned marriage she told me to get stuffed and left once again.

You must wonder why I put up with it. The answer is I love her. I suppose she enjoys the power she has over me. She left me again a week ago. She doesn't ring and when I ring her, her mother says she's gone out which I'm sure isn't true.

She's not one for a good time, for pubs or discos. She likes TV, reading and making love – pursuits we share. Can you explain her weird behaviour and tell me what I can do about it?

Says Marje

I admit I am as puzzled as you are. But what puzzles me most is that in a relationship that has gone on for three years you don't appear to have asked your girlfriend for a rational explanation of what seems highly irrational behaviour.

You say you are easy-going and I reckon that's putting it mildly. You are a total softie to put up with this humiliation – unless you unconsciously enjoy being humiliated.

I suppose her absences are a test of the strength of your love. She will, I guess, push you to the limit and it depends more on how much you can take as to how much longer you can take it.

There's one small clue in your letter that had me wondering. You say you "offered" to marry her. That sounds pretty patronising and I'm not surprised she told you to get stuffed.

Women prefer to be asked. A man ought to be sensitive enough to make a proposal sound like he hopes she'll say yes, rather than a reluctant offer she can take or leave.

It seems like you are reaching end-of-tether time. But you're not tough enough to tell your girlfriend she must either stay put or move out for good. She knows that it will take a lot of goading before you tell her enough is enough.

The sad thing is that if you did, it could well do the trick. If she really believed she was losing you she might even take you up on that offer. But will you take the risk? Could you?

Think about it. For if you continue to do nothing but make phone calls she refuses to answer, to make her welcome when she walks back in – she will continue to make the rules and play the game her way and you will always hold the losing card.

Desires of a mean man

Dear Marje

I am writing this to let off steam. I am so angry with my husband I feel like bashing him but it's safer to write to you.

We have been married for 22 years and until a year ago, I did full-time clerical work. He has a good job and we've got a nice home and two sons.

The trouble began when I lost my job and became dependent on my husband. He's always been tight with money but while I was earning a salary, it was never an issue. Now it is.

He resents handing over cash, even for our keep, let alone for my personal needs. I have to write down the cost of every item, down to tampons and tights.

He accuses me of being lazy because I won't look for work. I have looked, but who wants to employ a woman of 47 in an office in these days of young girls with high-tech skills. He treats me like a paid slave and a whore from whom he demands unacceptable practices. If I refuse, he docks my money. I know I'm stuck with him. At my age, what choice do I have?

Says Marje

I'm glad you diffused your anger by writing to me instead of wielding the frying pan over your husband's head. I can only admire your fortitude. You've got a very nasty one there. As a husband, he rates the lowest possible score.

Meanness with money usually goes hand in hand with meanness of spirit. He is bloody mean, with knobs on. And distinctly unpleasant.

His attitude to sex is particularly revolting and his unacceptable practices, whatever they are, do indeed put you in a similar position to women who submit to sex for money.

I use the word submit in your case, for professional whores willingly perform whatever acts their clients request.

Although you get paid, you are an unwilling participant and my advice to you is to tell your hateful husband to get lost. I can see why walking out might be difficult. You don't mention your sons' ages but if they're old enough to fend for themselves, don't let protective maternal feelings prevent you from considering your own.

It's true that another office job might be hard to come by, but don't run away with the idea that at the age of 47 you have no future. There are jobs to be picked up for those who are presentable, sensible and experienced.

A cleaning job would be honourable and preferable to the one you now do for free and would give you a modicum of independence. At least you'd be able to pay for your tampons and tights without begging from him. Try to be more assertive. Refuse to submit to slavery and near-prostitution. Go out now and then with a friend and let him cook his own supper. If he realises you are serious about resisting his demands there's a chance this mean man will think again about his treatment of a wife he'd be a good deal poorer without.

Back-to-work wife loses her homely touch

Dear Marje

When I got married four years ago, most of my friends

envied me. Their wives and girlfriends were into power-dressing and being successful and independent.

All my wife wanted was to give up her job – she'd been an estate agent – and be a housewife.

Then a couple of months ago she announced she was going back to her old job.

Since she started work again she has become a different person, bolshie and bossy and running the house like it's a penance. She forgot my birthday and now she's talking about taking a break from our marriage to find her own space, as she calls it.

I may have taken her for granted in the past but she's unfair when she said I liked seeing her as a domestic drudge.

She's breaking the bargain she made when we married, but I'd give anything for us to be happy again, if only I could see a way through this maze of problems.

Says Marje

The only way through your difficult maze, I think, is for you to come to terms, if you can, with the fact that the woman your wife is now is never going to go back to being the meek little helpmate you married.

She is an entirely different person and you are on a loser if you can't accept that. Maybe you don't even want to. In which case see a solicitor about giving your marriage a peaceful end.

I can't guess why she suddenly got tired of her housewife role. Clearly it didn't satisfy her need for independence.

There are still some women who enjoy being what they often describe as "mere" housewives. But your wife, truly believing at the beginning of your marriage that she wanted a quiet domestic life, found she needed more than that to sustain her mind and never mind about your body.

Understandably, you feel cheated at finding yourself tied to this stranger. But I think you'd be wise to encourage her desire to have her own space.

Perhaps when she's on her own and can look at her marriage from a safe distance she'll decide she'd rather come back to you – on HER terms I'm afraid – than leave you forever.

But before she goes you'll have to admit that you can see why you should compromise, as you must if you want to stay married. What I find hard to understand is how any man can try to persuade a woman that she ought to be content, even thankful, to be a domestic drudge.

Why, I wonder, didn't you spot the bitter resentment that was building up? Complacent, weren't you?

What you must do now is encourage her ambitions at work and make sure you do your fair share at home. That's the only way you'll ever get through to the end of that maze.

She'd love to be in control

Dear Marje

At 32, I have a well-paid, responsible job, I run the home I've shared with my partner for six years and I have two children.

I can make my own decisions yet I have never been allowed to.

My father has always treated me like a child. My brother bullied me and my partner makes all the family decisions. Not just the major ones, but trivial ones like which TV programmes we watch.

I meekly kow-tow to my employer. My children are bossy, although their father says I'm letting my imagination run wild.

I've tried to rebel but I've soon come to heel again. My women friends are strong and self-assertive and I despise myself for my weakness.

How can I stop people taking me over? Maybe you'll think this question, in itself, is a confession of defeat.

Dear Marje

All the major influences in your life have been men. You don't mention a mother or a grandmother or a sister who could have given you a sense of feminine worth.

It's difficult to guess why you need to be controlled by men. And puzzling as to why you now resent these controls.

I suppose it began with your father whose pet you clearly were. And a brother took over the control role as you both matured. Then you got a boss who, it seems, makes it plain he is one and then you fell in love with another hard, strong man who makes you watch Channel Four when you yearn to switch to Carlton or whatever.

I do not think you are genuinely rebellious. you simply believe you ought to be. Many women happily submit to decision-making men. Likewise there are plenty of "yes-dear" men, contentedly letting women take control. But because you are a competent and intelligent female, you feel it's time you told these bossy men and your bossy kids where they get off.

Don't do it. Don't fight it, or them. For you will never win. You were conditioned from an early age to defer to men and you've done pretty well out of being submissive.

If you start to fight your partner now for your right to choose which telly prog to watch, where you'll go for the hols and what you'll eat for dinner, you could spoil a good life just to make a point.

And the point I must make is that if you do alienate this present partner, you can be certain you'll come under the equally powerful control of the next one.

That's the kind of woman you are and you'd be less resentful if you could accept yourself for what you are – a woman who prefers strong men to weak wimps.

A wife's love for a bully

Dear Marje

When I read about the victims of bullying, I know exactly how frightened they must feel. I am one, too. Well-educated, aged 35, with three young children, I gave up a good job when I married because my husband insisted I stayed home. I loved him too much to struggle for my independence.

He has never abused me physically, only verbally. He lashes me with his tongue and the mental cruelty is unbearable.

After 12 years, I cower when he walks into the room. I spend hours in the kitchen alone, anything rather than endure his shouting and abuse. You won't be surprised to

hear I've started drinking, secretly. But while alcohol deadens the feelings a bit, the problem remains. I can't leave him because of the children. I have no money and I'd hate to burden my elderly parents. Can you see any answer for me?

Says Marje

There can't be an easy answer to this appalling problem except to walk away from it which, in your case, isn't practicable.

When I was a kid, bullied and badmouthed by other kids, my mother told me to stand up to them. But sound though this advice may have been, it doesn't work.

It didn't surprise me that you'd sought comfort from the bottle and it won't surprise you if I urge you to try to give it up.

I know a cup of tea is not as comforting or anaesthetising as a large gin but it's very important at this stage to maintain control.

I am tempted to suggest that you shout back when your husband shouts at you, but who knows how he'd respond? The verbal abuse might change to violence. He knows what a soft target you are.

I doubt if he attempts to bully colleagues or friends he meets in the pub. But he gets real pleasure, even perhaps a sexual kick, out of seeing you cowering in fear in the kitchen.

I am reluctant to remind you of that old saying "sticks and stones will break my bones but words can never hurt me". I'd hate you to think I was being flippant.

But if only you could manage to develop a thick skin and simply shrug and ignore his abuse, you'd be able to cope with it more easily.

He enjoys bullying you because your frightened response reinforces his power over you. A show of indifference hopefully would reduce that power.

I know, as well as you do, that escape is really the only answer. Perhaps you'd be less of a burden to your parents than you fear. You might be able to stay with them until you could get yourself sorted out. I can't see any other option than getting away from this bully before he finally destroys you.

He drives her crazy

Dear Marje

The day I passed my driving test two years ago, my delighted husband took me out to a celebration champagne dinner.

He drank a toast to me, saying that from then on, when we went out I could drive him so he could have a few drinks. He's always been careful about drinking and driving.

It suited me fine and it worked out just like he said. But I'm beginning to wish I'd never put my hands on the steering wheel.

He sits in the passenger seat and he never stops telling me what to do and how to drive. He warns me about pedestrian crossings and traffic lights ahead. He shouts at me if I cut a corner or if he thinks I'm too close to the vehicle in front.

He behaves like I'm a five-year-old instead of 25. He makes me so nervous, I'm terrified I'll have an accident.

When I drive on my own, I'm confident and careful. When he drives, he's very aggressive. Even writing about him winds me up. Help wanted, please.

Says Marje

A lot of men used to write to me about their pain-in-the-rear back-seat drivers who drove them bonkers. Mothers-in-law, usually, but there were plenty of wives, too, who couldn't keep their mouths shut.

Now that large numbers of women drive, they're getting a taste of what men had to put up with for years.

What's particularly infuriating for you is that your jabbering spouse wanted you to pass your test only for his own selfish ends.

I can offer one or two ideas. One is for you to announce, next time you set off for an evening out, that you are in the mood for a few drinks and he'll have to drive.

And on the way, give him the treatment he hands out to you and tell him why you won't drive again while he's in the car.

Another idea is to turn up the volume on the car radio and simply drown out his voice. The only snag with both of these suggestions is that they could lead to more rows once you got home.

I think your best bet is simply to be more assertive and tell him to belt up and let him see you mean it.

Somehow, though, I fear you are not a self-assertive type, otherwise you wouldn't have endured this bossy behaviour for two years, not even for two weeks.

I don't know what you'd call the female equivalent of a henpecked husband, but you, I think, are whatever it is. But don't despair or weep tears of frustration. You can actually take lessons in how to be assertive.

Call round at your local evening classes and enquire if they run courses. If they don't, I'm sure they'll be able to point you in the right direction.

Golly, I sound like your old man!

You passed your driving test okay and now it's time to show him he's got lessons to learn, too.

Lout she can't live without

Dear Marje

I am living with my boyfriend and I know that he loves me and our baby, but to him I just can't do a thing right.

My troubles started when I had my baby. My boyfriend and I split up just before I went into hospital and he didn't contact me until our son was two months old.

When I saw him again I begged him to give me another chance. I promised I'd do everything he asked and I said I'd never annoy him again. Now he's holding me to my promise. I'm not allowed to argue. If I do he says he'll find someone else who'll obey him.

I can't speak unless I'm spoken to. He frequently threatens to hit me and he calls me foul names.

One of his "punishments" is to phone his ex-girlfriend and make me listen.

My parents are begging me to go back home. They are worried about my safety.

But have I the right to deprive my son of a father, even though he treats me so badly?

No one would dispute that you are a fool to love this man. But cool reason and wisdom disappear when passion takes a person over. You know he is a cruel and spiteful lout, liable to beat you up if you fail to be meek and submissive.

But the power he has over you is stronger, even, than your fear of him. What's more, I don't believe that he loves you. If he does, why did he desert you when you were at the point of giving birth to his child?

He didn't seek the reconciliation. You did.

And when you made those absurd promises, he knew he'd have a willing victim for his sadistic practices.

I particularly dislike his emphasis on your obedience to him. And although you don't mention it, I'd like to bet he demands sexual obedience from you with the demeaning practices that go with such demands – even perhaps, bondage.

It would be foolish of me to encourage you to be more assertive towards him, to defy him.

I doubt very much if you could do it. And if you did find the courage to oppose him, he'd be determined to show you his superior strength – the strength to beat you up.

You are very lucky indeed to have such great parents to turn to and turn to them you should. The reason you give for hesitating is a feeble one. You doubt your right to deprive the baby of his father. But as his mother it's your duty to protect your son from a brutal man.

I guess you won't want me to urge you to leave the man you love, but urge I must. If your lover does indeed love you enough to want to try to rebuild your lives together, he'll come after you.

And if you ever do go back to him, make sure you don't make impossible promises you wouldn't be able to keep.

Husband who makes her feel like a has-been

Dear Marje

My husband and I are both 48. He treats me like I'm an

ageing has-been, but he describes himself as "distinguished".

He sneers at my looks and my clothes and says I have no style. He boasts about the girls at his office fancying him. When we go anywhere together he ignores me.

I'm grateful for my two sons and at last the worm is turning. Recently, he was away for three weeks and I really surprised myself, chatting away in the shops and going to the pub for a drink. People seemed to like me, including two or three men I met. Then my husband came home and, of course, I was my miserable, old, ugly, boring self again.

I don't know why I stay with him. This is the first time I've ever told anyone the truth about my marriage.

Says Marje

I don't know why you stay with him either. Doing a bit of mental arithmetic, I figure that your sons are probably young men now.

You, though undoubtedly cowed after years of being put down by your unpleasant spouse, are still young enough to get some enjoyment out of what has been a very joyless life.

Perhaps what has prevented you escaping from this sadistic man is that he provides you with a home.

You must have been a very submissive woman to have stayed in a marriage that has destroyed what little self-esteem you may once have had.

I wonder what caused your sudden impulse to rebel. Women in their menopausal forties do, literally, have a change of life.

For some it's a change for the worse, although it needn't be now that hormone replacement therapy is available.

For you though, it looks like a change for the better. And good for you.

Whatever it was that made the worm turn, you are now in a healthier position to contemplate your future.

You know you are attractive to men and I guess you would soon find one.

Without the dark shadow of your husband looming over you, you would feel much more relaxed and confident.

You must decide if you could survive without him.

Several readers of this column castigated me recently

because I advised a wife married to a disagreeable, grumpy man to stay with him. Why, asked these angry readers, didn't I advise her to get out?

That wife was incapable, I believed, of supporting herself and may very well have finished up homeless. I was convinced that she would not be able to cope on her own.

But you would be able to. Your sons must know how their father treats you. And if you fear that splitting from him could harm them, forget it. They'll be off soon enough, leading their own lives, if they haven't already gone.

And don't change the style your husband so contemptuously dismisses. Plainly, discerning people admire it.

The selection of letters published in this book were chosen from some of the anonymous letters I have received over the past few years. Some people are nervous, for a variety of reasons, of revealing their identity. But most people seeking confidential help tell me their names and addresses. If anyone reading this has a problem they believe I could solve, please write to Marje Proops, Mirror Group Newspapers, 33 Holborn, London EC1P 1DQ and I will do my very best to help. And all letters will remain strictly confidential.

17 T
28 THO